THE CHURCH IN CRISIS

ROBERT GRIFFITH

GRACE AND TRUTH PUBLISHING
PO Box 338, Gunnedah NSW 2380 Australia
www.graceandtruthpublishing.com.au

ISBN 978-1-7635504-4-5

TABLE OF CONTENTS

1. INTRODUCTION

Why are you reading this book? I doubt it's because my title is inspiring or captivating. I struggled for some time before settling on this title because I am not part of the growing cohort of church-bashing critics who delight in telling us what is wrong with the church. This book is not a list of the church's faults; nor is it an attack on the church. Quite the opposite, in fact. The church is in crisis because it is under attack on many fronts, and I want us all to wrestle with the reality of these attacks and find ways to conquer the various enemies within and without.

If you know any church history at all, you will understand that Christianity, from its inception to the present day, has never prospered for any significant period of time without experiencing a major crisis of some kind. Every one of these crises resulted in a significant portion of believers, both individuals and sometimes congregations, losing their way. Apostasy has occasionally been so pervasive that the New Testament church has essentially vanished from the historical record for considerable periods of time.

The apostasy that followed the death of the early Apostles, and eventually gave rise to Catholicism, was caused by what the Apostle Paul called, *"the secret power of lawlessness"* (2 Thessalonians 2:7), which was already in play before the first generation of Christians died. The church documented from the middle of the second century to the 'Reformation' in the 1500's was primarily an apostate church.

This does not imply that there were no local churches at all during that time who followed New Testament teaching. In fact, I've come across some data over the years that would suggest there may have been several faithful gatherings of orthodox believers throughout those dark years.

Secular and religious historians would not have seen them, which is why we don't read about them in any of the normal journals, but I am confident they were there.

From the Reformation until the present, numerous effective attempts have been made in the world to restore the faith of the New Testament times, with varying degrees of success. It doesn't matter where we are in the world, as long as we have the seed of the kingdom, which is the Word of God, we can teach and live out the gospel of Jesus Christ and produce Christians and churches that belong to and follow the Lord at any time and in any location.

We also have assurances in the Bible that God's kingdom will never be destroyed (Daniel 2:44) and that the Word of God will always endure (Matthew 24:35; 1 Peter 1:23-25).

In the United States, for example, a broad return to the New Testament order resulted from the 'Restoration Movement' that started in the early nineteenth century, while its earliest roots can be traced back to the eighteenth century.

This 'back to Bible' movement quickly gained traction across the country and the zeal for evangelism became very strong. Local churches were being established without regard to denomination, and many were baptised. There was a strong and sincere sense of unity among those who shared a similar commitment to New Testament truth.

Once more, a recognisable portion of God's people were working hard. From the pulpits of local churches that met in private homes, school buildings and small buildings they had constructed or purchased, the old gospel message was clearly being heard. However, the church was once more experiencing a crisis by the middle of the century.

A significant number of believers had come to realise that unless they pooled their resources and their energies into a working arrangement bigger than a local church, the grand job of evangelising the world would never be completed. Many agreements were therefore established where local churches and private Christians combined their funds.

In 1849, this effort developed into the *American Christian Missionary Society*, a national organisation. The local church was the only Biblical functioning organisation to carry out the church's ministry, according to brethren who rejected these structures and societies from the start.

Then for the remainder of the nineteenth century, believer's attention was largely focused on this tension. The topic was discussed in debates; articles were published; and sermons were delivered. The problem of new music in worship was also introduced during that time. A remnant of the church remained loyal to the old order, but the bulk of the church followed the new innovators, as had happened during the massive apostasy that followed the Apostles' deaths.

Generally speaking, churches who chose to not support the new music and the changes which were coming were less wealthy than those that did. As a result, very few churches could afford to hire full-time preachers to assist them in the early 1900s. Most of the preachers at the time barely had enough money to cover their expenditures when preaching on Sundays and during gospel meetings. During the week, they had to earn a living by farming or some other trade.

However, during the first part of the century, the churches expanded rapidly and thousands of people were baptised. Seldom did a gospel gathering end without a number of people expressing their faith in Christ and presenting for baptism.

The 'remnant' had expanded and thrived by the end of World War II. Many rural congregations had preaching every Sunday, while the majority of churches in cities and towns had full-time pastors. New Testament Christianity was certainly gaining momentum once again.

The 1950s and 1960s followed and ushered in yet another significant catastrophe. Similar to previous crises, the issues were debated, addressed in papers and from pulpits before the liberal/institutional and conservative/non-institutional churches were finally separated. Like before, most of the brethren followed the innovators and have since adopted more liberal doctrine and practices.

However, the conservative/non-institutional brethren not only survived but also expanded and thrived across the America, despite the pessimistic forecasts of their more liberal counterparts. As a result, not only in America, but in many nations, New Testament Christianity is still thriving.

Sadly, I believe the church is currently experiencing another serious crisis as we enter the second quarter of the twenty-first century. I am confident that the church will survive the storm in the long run and that a remnant will continue once more, however, in the near future, I think we will face some challenging times that will really put our faith to the test.

Hence the less than positive title of this book: *The Church in Crisis*. Many people want to ignore the realities I will be unpacking here, but we do so at our own peril. The current crisis engulfing the church is actually caused by a number of seemingly unrelated crises that threaten the fundamental foundation of the church.

In this book I have identified what I believe are the nine most serious issues which have always been present in the church but have intensified significantly in recent times.

The result is we now have a church which is in shackles as we try desperately to move forward in response to the call of God – only to be held back and rendered powerless by these serious enemies within.

Now just because I can, you will notice on the contents page, I have chosen words beginning with 'D' to describe each of the crises which need our serious attention if we are to embrace the call of God and join with Jesus in building a church against which even the gates of hell will not prevail. Some of these issues present in different ways and I want to explore how each manifestation can be identified and then, by God's empowering, overcome. The first step in resisting and defeating any enemy is identifying them clearly first.

I am confident that God will empower us to rise above each of these serious roadblocks and barriers. However, my fear is that too many believers are completely oblivious to the many dangers in our midst.

My hope and prayer in writing this book is to open people's eyes and give them hope for the future - a future where the church Jesus promised to build emerges triumphant and the church we have tried to build in our own strength, fades away.

I encourage you to come with me now on this journey of discovery, praying always that God's Spirit will speak truth to you, give you hope and show you a way forward in the midst of these very challenging times.

2. DISTRACTION

There seems to be a hundred distractions around me as I sit at my desk preparing to write this important chapter. Some are external, like the traffic in my street; the sound of sirens in the distance, which is triggering multiple dogs to howl. Other distractions are inward: I wonder what's going on in the news; is there anything in my inbox; which book should I read next; oh look, there's an ant climbing up my wall; yes, I am little hungry ... and on they go!

I know I'm not alone; everybody faces distractions. We all have our own issues that seek to divert us from focussing on the most important things in life. This is not only true at an individual level, the same is true at the organisational level. After all, individuals make up every organisation, be it a church, a business, a family, or a government agency. Imagine how simple it is for a huge group of individuals to become sidetracked from the goal for which that particular organisation exists.

Mission creep is the term being used today to characterise this phenomenon. It was first used for military operations, but it has since been employed in a variety of organisations and groups. Mission creep is referring to an organisation's propensity to progressively expand or change its goals and objectives beyond its original aim and purpose.

We could discuss mission creep from a purely practical standpoint if we were discussing any normal organisation. Naturally, it is not good for an organisation to stray from its initial purpose. This ultimately will hurt the organisation, particularly in the charity sector. The mission becomes too complicated and eventually unachievable; resources are overextended; and eventually the primary purpose is lost.

However, when it comes to the church, each of these points is equally valid. No church wants to overstretch its finances, divert attention from its main purpose, or make its mission unnecessarily difficult. When the church begins to engage in mission creep, the danger becomes greater. After all, the church has a unique mission – it is the mission of Christ.

According to Matthew 28:19–20, our mission is to make disciples, baptise them, and teach them all that there is to know about life and godliness in Christ Jesus. The gospel lies at the heart of that mission. The mission is impossible to achieve without the gospel. Mission creep happens at the gospel level when the true gospel is undermined, redefined or corrupted in some way. The true gospel is what makes the church special, strong, and ultimately unstoppable.

The church has been susceptible to mission creep since its inception. The temptation to condense the mission of Christ into some kind of culturally acceptable package was even a reality in the days of the early church. For example, the city of Corinth, the Greek equivalent of Rome, was a nexus of Hellenistic culture and ideas. It was a place where oratory skills were highly valued and a variety of different human philosophies continually fought for supremacy. That's why the apostle Paul wrote these words to the believers in that city, reminding them of their primary purpose:

> **1 Corinthians 1:17** *"Christ did not send me to baptise but to preach the gospel, and not with words of eloquent wisdom, lest the cross of Christ be emptied of its power."*

Paul saw the risk right away. In a place like Corinth, how would anyone make the church and its mission relevant? Oratory was a favourite pastime in that city. They cherished philosophy, wisdom, and well-spoken language. To them, the gospel was not any of these things.

It lacked eloquence. It wasn't 'smart.' Actually, it was seen as 'folly' (1 Corinthians 1:18). In Corinth, mission creep would signify something much more significant than being overburdened. It would include presenting the gospel as 'wise' in accordance with worldly wisdom.

Paul claims that this would render the gospel completely ineffective! With a message based on human intelligence and wisdom, the church was sure to win a lot of people, so many in Corinth believed.

It is this battle with humanism which so clearly spotlights the gospel, because the gospel has never been based on human knowledge. It is actually completely contrary to all human wisdom. In fact, human sensitivities are offended by the gospel, for obvious reasons.

The gospel calls us all to come before God naked, holding only our sin; it destroys every semblance of pride and self-worth; it forces us to acknowledge that we are powerless to alter our relationship with God; it exhorts us to place our sin at the feet of Jesus, Who took on human form, died, rose from the grave, and then ascended into the heavens.

That kind of messaging doesn't gain you many followers in the world of human wisdom, or so we might think. This is where it is all rather intriguing. People continue to believe! When they do, you can be sure it's not because the message they heard resonated with their human wisdom. Only God's power can achieve that outcome.

Paul knew there would be no power in the cross of Christ if he had come to Corinth preaching a gospel using poetic words of wisdom. When people accept the message despite its offensiveness, it demonstrates the power of the gospel.

1 Corinthians 1:18-21 *"For the message of the cross is foolishness to those who are perishing, but to us who are being saved it is the power of God. For it is written: "I will destroy the wisdom of the wise; the intelligence of the intelligent I will frustrate."*

Where is the wise person? Where is the teacher of the law? Where is the philosopher of this age? Has not God made foolish the wisdom of the world? For since in the wisdom of God the world through its wisdom did not know him, God was pleased through the foolishness of what was preached to save those who believe."

1 Corinthians 2:1-5 *"When I came to you, I did not come with eloquence or human wisdom as I proclaimed to you the testimony about God. For I resolved to know nothing while I was with you except Jesus Christ and him crucified. I came to you in weakness with great fear and trembling. My message and my preaching were not with wise and persuasive words, but with a demonstration of the Spirit's power, so that your faith might not rest on human wisdom, but on God's power."*

Paul's strict adherence to the gospel message is telling. His undivided focus is such a powerful example that the church should always follow. Too many distractions exist which seek to lead the church away from its primary purpose. A growing number of people in the church today inevitably believe they can enjoy these diversions while maintaining the strict tenets of gospel integrity in the hopes that it will increase the relevance, significance, and productivity of the church and its mission.

Throughout church history, distractions have led so many astray, ultimately because of the church's inability to trust in the gospel's unique ability to save.

It appears to the carnal mind that the gospel is insufficient. The New Testament writers all believed the world's pivotal moment had already occurred. By sending His Son, God showed His love for the world; condemned sin in the body of Jesus; poured out all of His wrath on Him at the cross; and brought about salvation via that final act of justice. Jesus was raised from the dead by God, and He then gave His disciples His mission, which is to spread the gospel and make disciples.

What steps did they take to fulfil this commission? They all essentially took the same action. None of them attempted to use political or educational institutions to carry out the mission of Christ. The book of Acts reports that they only explained to people - individually or in groups - who God is, what He has done in Jesus, and what this meant for them. The implication for every listener of the message is that they will either believe and be saved or they won't.

Human wisdom would suggest that there is a plethora of other things the church could be doing at this very moment that would be far more appealing and relevant to the world. That has always been the case.

Tragically, the church has always been skilled at chasing these diversions at the expense of the one thing that makes it special, strong, and unstoppable: sharing the gospel.

Political equality, morality, and social justice all seem like causes that would support the church in fulfilling its goal. They won't – not ever! The gospel is self-sufficient. Paul made this abundantly clear in his letter to the Romans.

> **Romans 1:16** *(The gospel is)* "... *the power of God for salvation to everyone who believes.*"

The gospel has more clout than any politician, government, or lobbyist. It penetrates the sinful, human heart, where no other agenda can.

There will be plenty more chances for the church to stand up for justice and decency as taught in the Bible. But let's be clear: **the church's mission cannot be confused with the gospel's results.**

Making disciples of all nations is the church's primary goal. There is only one message that accomplishes that goal, and whether or not the church thinks that message is enough to fulfil its mandate will be made abundantly evident. Like Paul, each of us must be prepared to speak to others with the determination and to *"know nothing among them but Jesus Christ and him crucified."*

In the next chapter, I will address some of the more serious distractions which have captured the minds and hearts of many Christians. They don't regard them as distractions at all – they are committed and enthusiastic and keen to see all believers embrace their beliefs and focus. I must warn you, however, that some sacred cows may be slaughtered in the pages which follow – so be prepared.

2. DISTRACTION (2)

There really are a multitude of distractions bombarding the church in these troubled times. I would need an entire book to unpack them all. However, I want to focus on just a few because I believe these are the ones which have led the people of God astray more than most. I also believe that if we can accept that these are dangerous and damaging to the effectiveness of the church and learn how to resist them and move past them, I truly believe the health of the church and the effectiveness of our mission will explode. So come with me now as I prepare to slaughter some sacred cows!

Social Action

The church today faces an unprecedented crisis - a crisis not from an external attack, but rather an internal deviation from its divine mandate. I am referring the rise of the 'Social Action' gospel, which prioritises humanitarian efforts and societal reform over the preaching of the true gospel of Jesus Christ.

While acts of charity and justice may have their place within Christian living, their elevation to the central purpose of the church has resulted in a dangerous distortion of biblical truth. The result is a church that is more concerned with temporal solutions than with the eternal salvation of souls.

The mission of the church is the mission of Christ Himself, and it is unmistakable. In what we have called the Great Commission; Jesus commands His followers:

> **Matthew 28:19-20** *"Go and make disciples of all nations, baptizing them in the name of the Father and of the Son and of the Holy Spirit, and teaching them to obey everything I have commanded you."*

This charge leaves no ambiguity: the primary work of the church is to proclaim the gospel, make disciples, and teach them to follow Christ. Nowhere does Scripture redefine this mission to focus on economic justice, political activism, or social change as an end in and of itself.

When the church replaces gospel proclamation with social activism, we shift our focus from the eternal to the temporal, losing sight of our divine calling. The apostle Paul warned us against any distortion of the gospel:

> **Galatians 1:8** *"But even if we or an angel from heaven should preach a gospel other than the one we preached to you, let them be under God's curse!"*

A redefined gospel that substitutes social activism for salvation through faith in Christ is really no gospel at all. The 'Social Action' gospel only misleads people by offering external change while neglecting the inward transformation that only the true gospel can bring.

Feeding the hungry and advocating for justice are noble pursuits, but when they replace the message of the cross, they become stumbling blocks rather than stepping stones to salvation.

Scripture calls Christians to good works, but always as the *fruit* of salvation—not as its *foundation*. What people fail to understand in their great passion for social action is that the power to achieve reform in all these areas lies in the gospel.

> **Ephesians 2:8-10** *"For it is by grace you have been saved, through faith - and this is not from yourselves, it is the gift of God - not by works, so that no one can boast. For we are God's handiwork, created in Christ Jesus to do good works, which God prepared in advance for us to do."*

The above verses make it clear that while good works are an expected result of salvation, they are not the mission itself. Yet many churches today have inverted this order, making social action the measure of a church's success rather than faithfulness to biblical teaching.

This subtle shift from gospel preaching to social reform may seem harmless at first, but it ultimately leads to a works-based religion that completely denies the sufficiency of Christ's atonement.

History bears witness to the tragic consequences of the church replacing gospel proclamation with social activism. The early 20th century saw many once-thriving churches abandon biblical preaching in favour of the 'Social Gospel' movement, which sought to bring about societal change while downplaying the need for individual salvation and transformation. The result was spiritual decay, as churches which once stood on the authority of Scripture soon became indistinguishable from secular humanitarian organizations. Jesus Himself addressed this tendency when He warned:

> **Mark 8:36** *"What good is it for someone to gain the whole world, yet forfeit their soul?"*

What use is feeding the hungry if their souls are never fed with the Bread of Life? What good is fighting for earthly justice if people die without embracing justification before God through Christ? The Church's calling is not to create a utopia on earth but to prepare people for eternity with God.

This is not to say that Christians should be indifferent to suffering or injustice. The Bible commands believers to care for the needy and seek the welfare of others. However, this concern for the needy must never overshadow or replace the primary mission of the Church.

The early Church was deeply engaged in acts of mercy, yet always only as a means to draw people to Christ, not as a substitute for the gospel. The apostle Peter, when he was confronted with a crippled man begging for alms, did not merely meet his physical need. Instead, he declared:

> **Acts 3:6** *"Silver or gold I do not have, but what I do have I give you. In the name of Jesus Christ of Nazareth, walk."*

Peter understood that the greatest gift he could offer was not material relief, but the power of Christ to transform lives. The modern church must recapture this perspective and embrace to the Gospel-centred mission of Christ. The only way for the church to address this crisis is to return to its biblical foundations. This requires four things:

A renewed commitment to preaching the true gospel …

Pastors and church leaders must prioritise sound doctrine over cultural trends and ensure that their congregations are nourished with the pure gospel of Jesus Christ.

A proper perspective on good works …

Acts of mercy and justice should always flow from gospel transformation and never replace the church's primary calling to make disciples of Jesus.

A call to repentance …

Many churches must repent for shifting their focus from Christ's commission to a worldly mission. Revival begins when the church is committed to the gospel of Christ.

Spiritual discernment …

Believers must be equipped to recognise when a movement, no matter how noble in appearance, is subtly leading the church away from its true purpose.

The only true hope for the world today is found in Jesus Christ, not in political reform, economic restructuring, or humanitarian efforts.

The church must once again be the light of the world - not by conforming to it, but by proclaiming the unchanging truth of the gospel boldly. Anything less is a distraction that leads people away from salvation and deeper into spiritual darkness.

> **2 Timothy 4:2** *"Preach the word; be prepared in season and out of season; correct, rebuke and encourage - with great patience and careful instruction."*

Inclusion

The church today faces another insidious crisis that comes not from external persecution, but rather from a dangerous internal compromise. The growing emphasis on so-called 'inclusion' has swept through our culture, affecting every sphere of society, including the church.

Under the banner of love, tolerance, and acceptance, many churches have now embraced a dangerous movement that directly contradicts the clear teaching of Scripture.

Issues surrounding sexuality, marriage equality, gender fluidity, and the uncritical embracing of anti-Christian cultures in our immigration policy have not only infiltrated public discourse but have also been granted legitimacy in pulpits that once stood firm on biblical truth. This insidious 'inclusion' movement is leading the church away from its unambiguous divine calling as it attempts to replace God's unchanging standards and truth with many ever-shifting ideologies of man. God's Word is clear that His people are to be set apart. The Apostle Peter reminds us:

1 Peter 1:15-16 *"But just as he who called you is holy, so be holy in all you do; for it is written: 'Be holy, because I am holy.'"*

Holiness is being 'set apart for God' and it is not an optional pursuit; it is the defining mark of the true church. Yet, the modern push today for 'inclusion' demands that believers abandon biblical truth in order to accommodate the world's standards and ideologies.

Almost daily I am being called to 'accept' lifestyles that the Bible explicitly condemns. This is not an act of love; this is simply spiritual compromise. The Apostle Paul warned us against such distortions of the faith:

2 Timothy 4:3-4 *"For the time will come when people will not put up with sound doctrine. Instead, to suit their own desires, they will gather around them a great number of teachers to say what their itching ears want to hear. They will turn their ears away from the truth and turn aside to myths."*

One of the most dangerous aspects of the current 'inclusion' movement is the redefinition of grace. Many have embraced the false idea that grace means unconditional affirmation of all choices, regardless of whether they align with God's Word. However, biblical grace will never ignore sin; it will call sinners to repentance. True grace always speaks truth. Jesus, who embodied grace *and* truth, did not hesitate to confront sin.

In John 8:11, when He encountered the woman caught in adultery, He extended grace but also commanded her, *"Go now and sin no more."* Grace and truth are inseparable in the gospel message. When churches preach a version of grace that excludes God's clear moral standards, they offer a counterfeit gospel.

One of the most prominent areas where 'inclusion' has undermined the Church is in the redefinition of marriage and sexuality. Scripture is unequivocal:

Genesis 2:24 *"That is why a man leaves his father and mother and is united to his wife, and they become one flesh."*

1 Corinthians 6:9-10 *"Or do you not know that wrongdoers will not inherit the kingdom of God? Do not be deceived: Neither the sexually immoral nor idolaters nor adulterers nor men who have sex with men... will inherit the kingdom of God."*

Despite the Bible's teaching, too many churches have caved in to cultural pressure, endorsing same-sex marriage, LGBTQ+ identities and gender fluidity as acceptable expressions of faith. In doing so, they deny the authority of Scripture and affirm lifestyles that lead people away from God's design.

Jesus Himself reinforced the biblical definition of marriage:

Matthew 19:4-5 *"Haven't you read," he replied, "that at the beginning the Creator 'made them male and female,' and said, 'For this reason a man will leave his father and mother and be united to his wife, and the two will become one flesh'?"*

When the church abandons this foundation, it ceases to stand as the pillar of truth and instead becomes complicit in the moral confusion of the age.

One of the most alarming developments in the 'inclusion' agenda is the promotion of gender fluidity, which denies the biological and biblical reality of male and female. This deception is rooted in rebellion against God's created order.

Genesis 1:27 *"So God created mankind in his own image, in the image of God he created them; male and female he created them."*

When the church embraces gender ideology, it departs from the truth that God intentionally designed humanity as male and female. The widespread acceptance of gender fluidity in some Christian circles is a rejection of God's authority as Creator. Rather than affirming those struggling with gender identity, the church must lovingly guide them toward the truth of who God created them to be.

Beyond sexuality and gender, the 'inclusion' movement has also affected the church's stance on immigration. While compassion for the foreigner is a biblical principle, many churches have adopted an uncritical acceptance of cultural influences that are hostile to Christian faith. This has led to a serious weakening of biblical values as churches prioritise political correctness over doctrinal purity. Scripture calls believers to extend hospitality but also to be discerning:

2 Corinthians 6:14 *"Do not be yoked together with unbelievers. For what do righteousness and wickedness have in common? Or what fellowship can light have with darkness?"*

The church needs to exercise wisdom in how it navigates immigration issues, ensuring that our commitment to inclusion does not welcome anti-Christian ideologies into our nation, to undermine biblical faith. This is especially true when we are dealing with those who embrace the Islamic faith. Most Christians in my country seem totally oblivious to the core teaching of Islam and this reflects in our lack of concern about the hundreds and thousands of Muslims who have been welcomed into our nation in just the last few years.

To Islam, we (Christians) are a blight on the earth. We are the 'infidel' and true Islamic followers are taught from birth to hate, despise and where possible, destroy all those who are not of the Islamic faith.

When the many Muslims in our nation now start running for local councils and state and federal governments, what do you think will happen to the Christian church? What decisions and policies will those authoritative bodies devise and approve when Islamic ideology emerges?

In the face of this 'inclusion' crisis, the church must return to its biblical foundation. This requires a commitment to Biblical truth; a true definition of love and grace; a clear stand on biblical morality; and a willingness to accept the criticism of many and face opposition. Remember that Jesus warned: us

> **John 15:18** *"If the world hates you, keep in mind that it hated me first."*

Standing for truth will bring opposition, but the church is called to fear God rather than man. The crisis of 'inclusion' is not about compassion or love - it is about truth versus deception. A church that prioritizes being accepted by the world over being faithful to God is a church that has lost its way. Now is the time for believers to be standing firm on the unchanging Word of God, refusing to bow to cultural pressure.

The only true hope for sinners - whether struggling with sexuality, gender identity, or any issue - is found in the transforming power of Jesus Christ.

It is my prayer that the church will rise to this challenge, rejecting the lies of 'inclusion' and embracing the eternal truth that sets people free.

John 8:32 *"Then you will know the truth, and the truth will set you free."*

End times speculation

Among the many distractions facing the modern church, one of the most persistent is an unhealthy obsession with end-times speculation. Countless believers are consumed by debates over the timing of Christ's return, the identity of the Antichrist; the nature of the tribulation; the meaning of the mark of the beast etc.

While the Bible does provide some teaching on the end times, the overemphasis on speculative interpretations has led many away from the church's primary mission: which is proclaiming the gospel, making disciples, and living faithfully for Christ each day. Jesus Himself warned against attempts to predict the exact timing of His return:

> **Matthew 24:36** *"But about that day or hour no one knows, not even the angels in heaven, nor the Son, but only the Father."*

Despite this clear statement, generations of Christians have speculated on the timing of the return of Christ. Many false predictions have led to disillusionment, fear, and even apostasy when the promised dates come and go and Jesus has not appeared. Instead of focusing on what Christ has commanded, faithfulness in the present, far too many are consumed by future events that are not meant to be fully understood this side of eternity. Rather than being fixated on signs and symbols, Jesus called His followers to be spiritually prepared:

> **Matthew 24:42** *"Therefore keep watch, because you do not know on what day your Lord will come."*

Readiness has nothing to do with deciphering prophetic codes; it's all about living a life of obedience, holiness, and proclaiming the gospel. When Christians become obsessed with identifying the Antichrist or interpreting all current events as signs of the apocalypse, they neglect the daily work of the kingdom of God.

Let me labour the point and remind you that Jesus left the church with a very clear mission:

> **Matthew 28:19-20** *"Therefore go and make disciples of all nations, baptizing them in the name of the Father and of the Son and of the Holy Spirit, and teaching them to obey everything I have commanded you."*

However, some people today are so preoccupied with end-times debates that they fail to evangelise, serve, or disciple anyone! The early church did not waste time speculating about the second coming - they spread the gospel with a sense of urgency, knowing that Christ's return was certain but its timing unknown.

Another danger of end-times speculation is the way it has been used to manipulate so many believers through fear. Sensationalist preachers and authors have capitalized on doomsday prophecies, creating a culture of panic rather than trust in God's sovereignty. The Apostle Paul warned against being unsettled by such alarmist messages:

> **2 Thessalonians 2:3** *"Don't let anyone deceive you in any way, for that day will not come until the rebellion occurs and the man of lawlessness is revealed."*

Rather than living in fear, Christians are called to trust God's plan and focus on faithful living.

One of the most frequently misused topics in end-times speculation is the debate about the 'mark of the beast' which is mentioned in Revelation 13. Every new technology, from barcodes to microchips, has been labelled as the mark of the beast, leading many Christians to panic unnecessarily.

However, Scripture teaches that the real danger is not a physical mark, but spiritual deception:

> **Revelation 13:16-17** *"It also forced all people, great and small, rich and poor, free and slave, to receive a mark on their right hands or on their foreheads, so that they could not buy or sell unless they had the mark, which is the name of the beast or the number of its name."*

The mark represents allegiance to worldly systems opposed to God, not merely a technological development. Instead of fearing each new advancement in technology, Christians should remain spiritually vigilant, ensuring their hearts remain loyal to Christ alone.

The Bible does talk about Christ's second coming, the final judgment, and the new creation. However, its primary message is one of hope and readiness, rather than fear and speculation. Paul's words to Titus provide the balance:

> **Titus 2:11-13** *"For the grace of God has appeared that offers salvation to all people. It teaches us to say 'No' to ungodliness and worldly passions, and to live self-controlled, upright and godly lives in this present age, while we wait for the blessed hop - the appearing of the glory of our great God and Savior, Jesus Christ."*

Christians should focus on living righteously, sharing the gospel, and trusting in God's timing rather than being consumed by speculative theories.

End-times speculation has become a dangerous distraction in the church, leading many away from their true calling. To be honest, my eyes glaze over and my stomach turns whenever a I hear a brother of sister speaking about the end times, like it is the most important thing we should all be discussing!

It is my firm belief that the Holy Spirit inspired all the teaching we have in the Bible. He also, I believe, inspired what was left out! 95% of the end-times speculation we hear and read today cannot be found in the Bible! I guess that's why they call it *speculation!*

Instead of trying to predict what is unknowable, believers should remain watchful, faithful, and dedicated to the mission of Christ. The return of Jesus is certain, but our responsibility is to live for Him *today*, knowing that in His perfect time, He will fulfill every promise.

> **Revelation 22:20** *"He who testifies to these things says, 'Yes, I am coming soon.' Amen. Come, Lord Jesus."*

3. DISCOURAGEMENT

There is a plague sweeping our nation and many others which is more pervasive than any other. It's not Covid or cancer, or the common cold. This plague, however, can be just as deadly as the most dreaded disease known to man. This plague is called discouragement.

Many things are true about discouragement. At least three things, however, make it a crisis in the church.

First of all, discouragement is universal. In other words, discouragement strikes everyone. None of us are immune to discouragement. Everyone you have ever known has been discouraged at one time or another. Wrack your brain as you may, you will not think of anyone who has avoided discouragement.

Young or old, rich or poor, educated or uneducated, black or white, red or yellow, advantaged or disadvantaged, non-Christian or Christian, everyone gets discouraged.

A second characteristic of discouragement is it's recurring. Being discouraged once does not give you an immunity to the disease. You can be discouraged over and over again. In fact, you can even be discouraged by the fact that you are discouraged! There is no antibody which can be injected which gives you immunity. Discouragement comes and goes, and it comes back again.

A third characteristic of discouragement is that it's highly contagious. Discouragement will spread fast by even casual contact. People can become discouraged because you are discouraged. You can become discouraged because other people are discouraged.

Often, when the enemy of God comes against us, we will become discouraged. It is important to know this, and to recognise it for what it is. If we understand just how this discouragement comes, then we might also understand how we can deal with this discouragement in a positive way. Discouragement will come. The challenge we have is to know the signs of its coming and the actions we must take to overcome it. We need to understand both the causes and the cures for discouragement.

Cause 1: Fatigue

You can probably think of any number of projects you have undertaken where you had to face the reality of fatigue. It might have been a project at work, or some project around your house. About half-way through the project, you began to think that you would never finish. Perhaps it was taking much longer than you thought, which happens to us all. Perhaps you began to rationalise and even develop various arguments for why you shouldn't finish. Maybe you even began to think that it wasn't God's will that you finish.

Many people fail to complete many things because of that kind of fatigue and discouragement. This is especially true when things are going wrong in the process. When you knock the paint over, or break the glass, or blow up the microwave you are trying to install, it can be discouraging. This is especially true when you are tired physically.

Cause 2: Frustration

Frustration is another reason why we become discouraged. At times we lose sight of our goal when we have so much other junk in our lives with which to deal. The rubbish in your life may be the sins of wrong deeds, or wrong thoughts or attitudes which you are unwilling to let go of.

Or the rubbish may be simply the many trivial things that waste your time, consume your energy, and spend your money. The junk or rubbish is anything which gets in our way, that keeps us from accomplishing the truly important goals in our lives. And the rubbish does one critical thing - it frustrates us. That is why we need to deal with the rubbish in our lives regularly. But we need first to understand that all this junk is a problem.

In Hebrews 12:1 we are told that we should *"lay aside every encumbrance."* Having a lot of rubbish in our lives is an encumbrance or weight. It slows us down. It trips us up. It causes us to stumble. It can make us fall. And it's very frustrating. It is like trying to run through a briar patch - there is simply no easy way to do it. The result is that we spend all of our attention and energy on the rubbish and never accomplish the primary goal. Frustration is a prime cause of discouragement.

Cause 3: Fear

Another major cause of discouragement is fear. Fear is very discouraging. When you are afraid, how do you respond? Well, sometimes it makes you just want to give up. If we feel like the task it too large and the resources too meagre, sometimes we will just give up for fear that we bit off more than we could chew.

We must be careful not to let fear overcome us. We must be aware that when we are fearful, we are also vulnerable to discouragement. This is a tactic of the enemy. It is one of his chief strategies in defeating us.

We have seen three things that can bring discouragement into our lives. Fatigue, frustration, and fear. Be on your guard when you encounter them. Wherever they are, discouragement is not far behind.

But what can we do about discouragement? We have seen some of the causes. What are some of the cures?

Cure 1: Reorganise & Refocus

If you have a problem, then reorganise and refocus on the main objective. Do you have a problem in your marriage? Well, don't quit! Change your approach, change your attitude. Reorganise your thought processes. Do you have a problem in your business? Don't give up! Change your priorities.

Do you have a problem in your walk with God? Don't stop following Jesus! Reorganise your prayer life. Surrender that area in your life you have been holding back. Perhaps you're frustrated by all the rubbish in your life. Reorganise it. Get rid of some of it. The point is - don't give up! Don't be overcome by discouragement. Do something about it!

Cure 2: Remember

In order to overcome discouragement, we must remember that the Lord is faithful. When Nehemiah faced opposition and saw the discouragement in his people when they were rebuilding the wall, he spoke to the nobles, the officials, and the rest of the people: *"Do not be afraid of them; remember the Lord who is great and awesome."*

How do you remember the Lord? What do you remember about Him? Well, you remember first that He is there! You can be very discouraged when you think you are all alone in the situation. But God is there! He is there whether you realise it or not, but it helps to realise it!

Next, you remember that God is great and awesome. God is sufficient to deal with your discouragement and with the situation you face.

When you are discouraged, you must turn your attention from your discouragement to the One Who is able to do something about your situation. God has been faithful to you in the past; He is faithful to you today; and He has promised to be faithful to you in the future. Remember the Lord. Remember His promises. Remember His goodness. Remember His power. Our God is an awesome God!

Cure 3: Resist

Finally, you must wage a battle against discouragement. You must be active and fight discouragement. It is clear from the Scriptures that we, as believers, are in a spiritual battle. We are engaged in a supernatural conflict and our enemy is the devil and his followers. Satan and his demonic spirits are totally committed to doing everything possible to discourage us and defeat us. We need to do precisely what Nehemiah encouraged the people to do. We must resist.

This is also what we are told to do in James 4:7. There we are told to "*Resist the devil.*" We are to resist his work in our midst. We are to resist his negative thoughts. We are to resist all of the discouragement that he tries to bring into our lives. We must fight the fight of faith and stand firm against the work of the enemy in our midst. Only then will we find success in our battle against discouragement.

Fatigue, frustration, and fear can bring discouragement, but reorganising our priorities, remembering our Lord, and resisting the devil can bring us through discouragement. If we apply these principles, God will always give us victory.

I think we often forget that even though the Bible warns us about the tough times we will endure as disciples of Jesus, God never wants us to accept discouragement as the 'norm' for our lives. We are meant to live above this and we can.

Biblical examples and lessons

The Bible is filled with examples of faithful men and women who faced discouragement yet overcame it through faith in God. By examining their stories, we can gain insight and encouragement for our own lives.

Moses: Overwhelmed by leadership ...

Moses is one of the most prominent figures in the Bible, yet he faced significant discouragement. Leading the Israelites out of Egypt was not an easy task at all. Despite witnessing miraculous signs, the people constantly complained and doubted God's provision. At one point, Moses cried out to God in frustration:

> **Numbers 11:14** *"I cannot carry all these people by myself; the burden is too heavy for me."*

Moses felt inadequate and overwhelmed by the weight of responsibility. However, God provided a solution by appointing seventy elders to help share the burden (Numbers 11:16-17). This teaches us that when we are discouraged by overwhelming tasks, seeking help and relying on God's provision can bring relief and strength.

Elijah: Despair after victory ...

Elijah, the great prophet, experienced an incredible victory over the prophets of Baal on Mount Carmel (1 Kings 18). However, immediately after, he faced fierce opposition from Queen Jezebel, who sought to kill him. Elijah fled into the wilderness and prayed:

> **1 Kings 19:4** *"I have had enough, Lord," he said. "Take my life; I am no better than my ancestors."*

Elijah's discouragement led him to despair and isolation. However, God responded by providing food, rest, and a renewed mission. He revealed Himself in a gentle whisper (1 Kings 19:11-12), not in a mighty wind or earthquake. This teaches us that even in our lowest moments, God sustains us and gently guides us forward.

Job: suffering and loss ...

Job endured such immense suffering – losing his children, wealth, and health in rapid succession. His friends even misunderstood him, and his wife advised him to curse God and die (Job 2:9). Job lamented:

> **Job 3:11** *"Why did I not perish at birth, and die as I came from the womb?"*

Despite his deep discouragement, Job refused to abandon his faith in God. In the end, God restored his fortunes and blessed him even more than before (Job 42:10). Job's story reminds us that even in the darkest times, perseverance and faith in God lead to restoration.

David: Betrayal and loneliness ...

David, the man after God's own heart, faced many moments of discouragement. One such instance occurred when he was fleeing from King Saul, who sought to kill him. He wrote:

> **Psalm 13:1** *"How long, Lord? Will you forget me forever? How long will you hide your face from me?"*

David felt abandoned and discouraged, yet he always turned to God in prayer. By the end of Psalm 13, David is declaring his trust in God.

Psalm 13:5 *"But I trust in your unfailing love; my heart rejoices in your salvation."*

David's example teaches us that when we feel forgotten or betrayed, we should pour out our hearts to God and remember His faithfulness.

Jeremiah: The weeping prophet …

Jeremiah was called by God to be a prophet during a time of great rebellion and unrest in Israel. He faced rejection, imprisonment, and ridicule. At one point, he lamented:

Jeremiah 20:14 *"Cursed be the day I was born! May the day my mother bore me not be blessed!"*

Jeremiah's discouragement was so intense, yet he found strength in God's promises. He declared:

Jeremiah 20:11 *"But the Lord is with me like a mighty warrior; so my persecutors will stumble and not prevail."*

His story reminds us that even when opposition surrounds us, God remains our defender and source of strength.

Peter: Failure and restoration …

Peter, one of Jesus' closest friends and disciples, faced deep discouragement after denying Christ three times (Luke 22:61-62). He wept bitterly, feeling the weight of his failure. However, Jesus later restored Peter, giving him a renewed purpose:

John 21:17 *"Feed my sheep."*

Peter's story teaches us that failure is never the end. God's grace is sufficient to restore and use us for His glory.

Paul: Opposition and hardship ...

The great apostle Paul endured relentless persecution, imprisonment, and hardship. Yet, he wrote:

> **2 Corinthians 4:8-9** *"We are hard pressed on every side, but not crushed; perplexed, but not in despair; persecuted, but not abandoned; struck down, but not destroyed."*

Paul found strength in Christ, declaring:

> **Philippians 4:13** *"I can do all this through him who gives me strength."*

Paul's resilience shows us that no matter how difficult our circumstances, we can press on through Christ's strength.

The Bible provides numerous examples of individuals who faced discouragement and yet overcame it through faith, perseverance, and total reliance on God. Whether feeling overwhelmed like Moses, despairing like Elijah, suffering like Job, betrayed like David, rejected like Jeremiah, failing like Peter, or enduring hardship like Paul, we can take comfort in knowing that God is always our strength.

When we encounter discouragement, let us remember these wonderful words from the prophet Isaiah:

> **Isaiah 40:31** *"But those who hope in the Lord will renew their strength. They will soar on wings like eagles; they will run and not grow weary, they will walk and not be faint."*

God remains faithful, and in Him, we can find the strength to overcome any discouragement.

4. DISSATISFACTION

It's the curse of our age! We have so much, but we want more. Even if we don't need it, and even if God has given no indication that He wants to give it to us, we still want it. When we are focused on what we *don't* have, it is just impossible to really appreciate and be grateful for what we *do* have! This leads us into dissatisfaction, and we now have an entire advertising industry which thrives on and feeds off our dissatisfaction.

Dissatisfaction is that feeling of discontent and displeasure with circumstances in life and/or other people. So, pause for a minute now, and think about what you *do* have. You would like to have more money – but how much money do you have? There are some things you would like to own – but what do you already own? Perhaps your physical health is limited – but what can you still do? How are you blessed with abilities that enable you to create beauty, with friends who bring richness to life, or with good memories that warm your heart in moments of solitude?

The secret to banishing dissatisfaction is not really a secret. We just don't want to embrace the secret because our fallen, broken human nature always seems to take pleasure in complaining! Gratitude is like a lens that helps us refocus our attention from our perceived lacks (which might not be good for us anyway) to our actual blessings from God. In this way, gratitude leads us into contentment and brings healing to our soul.

When Christ fills our heart and mind, we can be at peace and content with the things, people, and circumstances our sovereign God has placed in our life and stop yearning for the things He has not given us or allowed us to have.

The only thing that truly will satisfy the human soul is knowing Jesus Christ. Striving, coveting, and spending our time wanting what is not available to us can often leave us broken, bitter and always dissatisfied. I want to encourage you to read on and seriously wrestle with what I am about to share with you. This is not an inconsequential issue. Dissatisfaction is a cancerous disease in our society and in the church and it wreaks havoc every moment it is allowed to control our thoughts, desires and attitude.

Some facts about dissatisfaction:

The enemy causes dissatisfaction ...

The Bible says in John 10:10 that it is the enemy that kills, steals, and destroys. If you are dissatisfied and unhappy, guess who stole your joy? Jesus came to destroy the work of the enemy and to give you abundant life. He wants you to be content and happy.

Disappointments cause dissatisfaction ...

Sometimes other people or circumstances disappoint you. At other times you disappoint yourself by failures. These disappointments can very often lead us into dissatisfaction. Dissatisfaction with your own performance or that of others around you leads to dissatisfaction, and dissatisfaction can lead to depression.

Materialism causes dissatisfaction ...

> **1 Timothy 6:9-10** *"People who want to get rich fall into temptation and a trap and into many foolish and harmful desires that plunge men into ruin and destruction. For the love of money is a root of all kinds of evil. Some people, eager for money, have wandered from the faith and pierced themselves with many griefs."*

All the things that you want which seem so important are usually only temporal. You really need to focus on what is eternal (1 John 2:15-17).

Dissatisfaction is sin ...

When you are dissatisfied, grumbling, and complaining, you are in effect blaming God for your bad circumstances, implying that He is not providing adequately for your needs.

Israel was repeatedly dissatisfied with God's provision in the wilderness. They grumbled about the lack of water and food. Then they complained because the manna God provided was not as good as the leeks and garlic they had back in Egypt. God said their grumbling was sin and judged it as such.

Dissatisfaction always leads to grumbling, complaining, unhappiness, an unthankful and even a critical spirit. There is nothing positive or helpful about dissatisfaction.

Dealing with Dissatisfaction

Recognize that dissatisfaction is sin ...

As with all sins, you must confess this sin and embrace God's forgiveness and healing.

Ask God to give you a spirit of contentment ...

> **Philippians 4:11-13** *"...I have learned to be content whatever the circumstances. I know what it is to be in need, and I know what it is to have plenty. I have learned the secret of being content in any and every situation, whether well fed or hungry, whether living in plenty or in want. I can do everything through him who gives me strength."*

Paul told young Timothy to be content with the basics of food and clothing (1 Timothy 6:8). The Hebrews were also admonished to be content with what they had.

Put your trust in God ...

Don't put your trust in other people or things that will fail (Psalm 20:7-8; 44:6; 146:3). Only trust in God. That way you will never be disappointed or dissatisfied.

Make positive changes in your life ...

What changes can you make that will eliminate negative circumstances in your life? What changes will bring joy back into your life? Think about this – there will be many.

Return to the basics of Christian life ...

Be faithful in prayer, church attendance, and meditating on the Word of God. The Word of God is effective to facilitate change in the midst of any problem or circumstance in your life. Dissatisfaction is a state of mind, and your mind can be renewed by God. (Rom. 12:1-2; Eph.4:23; Col. 3:10).

Cultivate friendships with positive people ...

Avoid being a loner. Satan wants to isolate you through dissatisfaction. You should deliberately spend time with believers who are positive and uplifting. Do not hang around with negative, critical, judgmental people – this will contribute to your dissatisfaction. Christian friendships with positive people will really help you when you feel discouraged (Ecclesiastes 4:9-10).

Do something for other people ...

This will take the focus off those things which may be causing your dissatisfaction. The joy you receive from doing acts of kindness towards others will really help you eliminate your dissatisfaction.

When you see how tough some other people have it, you may also be more satisfied with your own lot in life.

Start a gratitude journal ...

Write down at least one thing each day for which you are thankful. This will help you remain focused on the positive instead of the negative. It is the will of God for you to give thanks in everything (1 Thessalonians 5:18).

Recognize the difference between happiness and true joy ...

Happiness is always based on outward circumstances. When things are going well, then you are happy. When circumstances are bad, you are unhappy. Joy, on the other hand, is a spiritual fruit from God. You can rejoice in every circumstance and the joy of the Lord gives you strength to face negative circumstances (Philippians 4:4, 1 Thess. 5:18).

Jesus faced the most difficult circumstances of His life with joy. Although He knew the suffering that awaited Him in Jerusalem, He entered the city with a joyous procession. In view of this, *"Let us fix our eyes on Jesus, the author and perfecter of our faith, who for the joy set before him endured the cross"* (Hebrews 12:2). Pray this every morning: *"Restore to me the joy of your salvation and grant me a willing spirit, to sustain me"* (Psalm 51:12).

What the Bible says about dissatisfaction

You may be surprised to learn that the Bible has a lot to say about the insidious cancer of dissatisfaction. I have selected just 31 references for you to study, but there are hundreds more. Why would the Bible have so much to say about dissatisfaction? The answer is simple. God knows we are broken, self-consumed and prone to look inward and not upward or outward.

Dissatisfaction reared its ugly head in the Garden of Eden and it has been a curse to us ever since. Therefore, God has a lot to say about dealing with this enemy of our souls.

I want to beg you, in Jesus' name, to not skim over these verses. As you read them, I implore you to listen for the voice of God to you today – right now – in your personal circumstances, which He knows only too well.

I could preach a sermon on each one of these passages – they are so important and so relevant today – especially for rich, affluent, blessed, but dissatisfied Christians in the modern world! Hear the Word of the Lord:

Nehemiah 8:10 *"… for the joy of the Lord is your strength."*

Psalm 37:3-4 *"Trust in the Lord and do good; dwell in the land and enjoy safe pasture. Take delight in the Lord, and he will give you the desires of your heart."*

Psalm 42:2 *"My soul thirsts for God, for the living God. When can I go and meet with God?"*

Psalm 63:1 *"You, God, are my God, earnestly I seek you; I thirst for you, my whole being longs for you, in a dry and parched land where there is no water."*

Psalm 63:5 *"I will be fully satisfied as with the richest of foods; with singing lips my mouth will praise you."*

Psalm 90:14 *"Satisfy us in the morning with your unfailing love, that we may sing for joy and be glad all our days."*

Psalm 91:16 *"With long life I will satisfy him and show him my salvation."*

Psalm 103:1-5 *"Praise the Lord, my soul; all my inmost being, praise his holy name. Praise the Lord, my soul, and forget not all his benefits – who forgives all your sins and heals all your diseases, who redeems your life from the pit and crowns you with love and compassion, who satisfies your desires with good things so that your youth is renewed like the eagle's."*

Psalm 107:9 *"… for he satisfies the thirsty and fills the hungry with good things."*

Psalm 145:16 *"You open your hand and satisfy the desires of every living thing."*

Isaiah 55:2-3 *"Why spend money on what is not bread, and your labour on what does not satisfy? Listen, listen to me, and eat what is good, and you will delight in the richest of fare. Give ear and come to me; listen, that you may live. I will make an everlasting covenant with you, my faithful love promised to David."*

Isaiah 58:11 *"The Lord will guide you always; he will satisfy your needs in a sun-scorched land and will strengthen your frame. You will be like a well-watered garden, like a spring whose waters never fail."*

John 4:13-14 *Jesus answered, "Everyone who drinks this water will be thirsty again, 14 but whoever drinks the water I give them will never thirst. Indeed, the water I give them will become in them a spring of water welling up to eternal life."*

Luke 6:21 *"Blessed are you who hunger now, for you will be satisfied …"*

John 6:33 *"For the bread of God is the bread that comes down from heaven and gives life to the world."*

John 6:35 *Then Jesus declared, "I am the bread of life. Whoever comes to me will never go hungry, and whoever believes in me will never be thirsty."*

John 7:38 *"Whoever believes in me, as Scripture has said, rivers of living water will flow from within them."*

John 10:10 *"The thief comes only to steal and kill and destroy; I have come that they may have life and have it to the full.*

John 15:11 *"I have told you this so that my joy may be in you and that your joy may be complete."*

Romans 14:17 *"For the kingdom of God is not a matter of eating and drinking, but of righteousness, peace and joy in the Holy Spirit ..."*

Galatians 5:22-23 *"...the fruit of the Spirit is love, joy, peace, forbearance, kindness, goodness, faithfulness, gentleness and self-control. Against such things there is no law."*

Philippians 4:4-9 *"Rejoice in the Lord always. I will say it again: Rejoice! Let your gentleness be evident to all. The Lord is near. Do not be anxious about anything, but in every situation, by prayer and petition, with thanksgiving, present your requests to God. And the peace of God, which transcends all understanding, will guard your hearts and your minds in Christ Jesus.*

Finally, brothers and sisters, whatever is true, whatever is noble, whatever is right, whatever is pure, whatever is lovely, whatever is admirable – if anything is excellent or praiseworthy – think about such things. Whatever you have learned or received or heard from me or seen in me – put it into practice. And the God of peace will be with you."

Philippians 4:11-13 *"I am not saying this because I am in need, for I have learned to be content whatever the circumstances. I know what it is to be in need, and I know what it is to have plenty.*

I have learned the secret of being content in any and every situation, whether well fed or hungry, whether living in plenty or in want. I can do all this through him who gives me strength."

Philippians 4:19 *"And my God will meet all your needs according to the riches of his glory in Christ Jesus."*

1 Thessalonians 5:16-18 *"Rejoice always, pray continually, give thanks in all circumstances; for this is God's will for you in Christ Jesus."*

1 Timothy 6:8 *"But if we have food and clothing, we will be content with that."*

1 Timothy 6:9-10 *"Those who want to get rich fall into temptation and a trap and into many foolish and harmful desires that plunge people into ruin and destruction. For the love of money is a root of all kinds of evil. Some people, eager for money, have wandered from the faith and pierced themselves with many griefs."*

Hebrews 13:5 *Keep your lives free from the love of money and be content with what you have, because God has said, "Never will I leave you; never will I forsake you."*

1 Peter 1:8-9 *"Though you have not seen him, you love him; and even though you do not see him now, you believe in him and are filled with an inexpressible and glorious joy, for you are receiving the end result of your faith, the salvation of your souls."*

2 Peter 1:3 *"His divine power has given us everything we need for a godly life through our knowledge of him who called us by his own glory and goodness."*

1 John 2:15-17 *"Do not love the world or anything in the world. If anyone loves the world, love for the Father is not in them. For everything in the world – the lust of the flesh, the lust of the eyes, and the pride of life – comes not from the Father, but from the world. The world and its desires pass away, but whoever does the will of God lives forever."*

The sins behind dissatisfaction

If you are not already squirming, then I must warn you: I am about to sharpen the point some more as I wrap up this important chapter. I have already established clearly that dissatisfaction is a sin, however, there are three primary sins which hide in the background and fuel this debilitating condition in us. Those three sins are pride, rebellion and unbelief. These are the original sins of the devil and his angels. They are sins that come from hell itself.

Dissatisfaction is a manifestation of **PRIDE**

> **Jude 16** *"These [the ungodly] are grumblers, malcontents, following their own sinful desires; they are loud-mouthed boasters, showing favouritism to gain advantage."*

Dissatisfaction is a manifestation of pride. It flows from a heart that says, *"I deserve better than God has given me."* This was the original sin of Satan himself.

In the letter of Jude, we have a reference to angels who, like Satan, were not content to be the servants of God, *"angels who did not stay within their own position of authority but left their proper dwelling."* (Jude 6).

Pride led some angels to say, *"We deserve better than God has given to us!"* God gave them positions of authority, but they were not satisfied. They are certainly not satisfied now. They never will be. Thomas Boston says, *"The devil is the proudest creature and the most dissatisfied because pride and discontent always live under one roof."*

If I catch myself thinking that I deserve better, I look in the mirror and say firmly, *"That is the opposite of everything you believe!"* I believe God has given me abundantly more than I ever deserved. What I deserve is death and hell. But God has loved me. God has given His Son for me. God has blessed me with every spiritual blessing in Christ. He has given me all that I need for life and godliness.

In all things His love surrounds me, and in all things, He pursues His great purpose, which is also my purpose, that a true likeness of His Son, Jesus Christ, be formed in me. Dissatisfaction is a hellish sin because it is a manifestation of pride.

Dissatisfaction is an expression of REBELLION

In the Old Testament, we have the story of Job, a good and godly man who was greatly blessed by God. His family was blessed, his business was blessed. Job was living the dream, and then one day through a series of disasters, he lost absolutely everything, in human terms. Job said, *"The Lord gave, and the Lord has taken away; blessed be the name of the Lord."* (Job 1:21).

The dissatisfied and discontent person says something different. They say, *"The Lord gave, but He should have given more,"* or, *"The Lord has taken away, and He should not have done that."* Jude talks about *"harsh things that ungodly sinners have spoken against God."* Dissatisfaction is a terrible sin because, at its heart, it represents rebellion against God.

The clay says to the potter, *"Why have you made me like this?"* (Romans 9:20). *"God, you should have done something different!"* That's rebellion, and the Scripture says, *"Who are you to speak like that to God?"* (Romans 9:20).

Dissatisfaction is a fruit of **UNBELIEF**

You see this is Exodus 17. God's people had been greatly blessed. He brought them out of slavery in Egypt, and He provided manna to feed them in the wilderness. Why is it that those who are most blessed are often most dissatisfied? Then God's people came to a place where there was no water. Now that is a legitimate concern and there are times in life when we may have legitimate concerns about how God will supply what we need. But their legitimate concern metastasized into unbelief. They tested the Lord by saying, *"Is the Lord among us or not?"* (17:7)

They were redeemed people, but they lost confidence that God was still with them. If you no longer believe that God is with you, you will no longer be confident that He will supply what you need.

Then it will not be long before the grumbling begins and you find yourself sliding right into dissatisfaction. I will deal with the issue of unbelief in more detail in chapter 7.

How then shall we live?

I really hope you are in a place where you can now say:

"I didn't think too much about this before, but now I see that I need to deal with this sin wherever it rears its ugly head in my life. I need to get beyond the idea that moaning and complaining always wanting more than I have doesn't really matter. I need to get serious about moving from anger to peace, from frustration to satisfaction, and from anxiety to trust."

Thank God there is a Saviour to Whom you can turn. Ask Him to help you deal with this sin if you see it in your life today. Ask Him to cleanse you afresh and wash this from your heart. Then ask Him to help flood your mind and your heart with a spirit of Godly contentment.

True satisfaction and peace in life comes from knowing that everything that concerns you is in the hands of the Saviour Who loves you. Satisfaction lies in knowing that in Jesus Christ you have everything you need. Trust begins when you know that He is faithful, and those who look to Him are never put to shame. Let me finish this chapter with an example from real life.

Actress Lori Loughlin was sentenced to two months in federal prison for her role in a college admissions scandal. Her husband, and co-defendant, received five months in prison and 250 hours of community service. During the hearings, US District Judge Nathaniel Gorton addressed Lori with these incredibly cutting, but insightful words:

"Here you are an admired, successful, professional actor with a long-lasting marriage, two apparently healthy, resilient children, more money than you could possibly need, a beautiful home in sunny Southern California – a fairy tale life. Yet you stand before me a convicted felon. And for what? For the inexplicable desire to grasp even more."

Our society has been taken captive by an inexplicable desire to grasp even more. We are blessed beyond measure. We enjoy a lifestyle which is the envy of most of the world and yet we still want what we don't have. This is a tragic place for any person to live, but for a disciple of Christ to find themselves in this pit of dissatisfaction – is, quite frankly, completely incomprehensible. We should actually be the most satisfied people on the planet.

Just imagine, if you can, how magnetic and dynamic the Church would be if everyone who followed Jesus could be free from the sin of dissatisfaction today? We would shine like spotlights in the darkness and depression of this dissatisfied, self-absorbed world.

That is our calling. That is our true destiny. That is what the world desperately needs us to be! Let those who have ears to hear, listen to what the Spirit is saying to the Church today.

5. DECEPTION

In these troubled times, one of the greatest crises facing the church is deception. Deception in the church today is not a distant concern; it is an urgent reality which is playing out in congregations across the world. Many well-intentioned believers have fallen prey to misleading doctrines, spiritual compromise, and manipulative leadership, very often with devastating consequences. Paul warned us long ago about this very issue when he was writing to the Corinthians.

> **2 Corinthians 11:3** *"But I am afraid that just as Eve was deceived by the serpent's cunning, your minds may somehow be led astray from your sincere and pure devotion to Christ."*

Deception is certainly not a new phenomenon; it has been Satan's tactic since the beginning. However, in our modern world, it seems that deception has taken on new and more insidious forms, drawing many away from the truth of the Gospel of Jesus Christ.

Deception through false teaching

The most obvious and dangerous form of deception which is infiltrating the church today is false teaching. Many churches have embraced teachings that deviate from the clear truth of Scripture. Paul's words to young Timothy are as relevant now as they were then:

> **2 Timothy 4:3** *"For the time will come when people will not put up with sound doctrine. Instead, to suit their own desires, they will gather around them a great number of teachers to say what their itching ears want to hear."*

False doctrines come in many forms. Some churches preach a prosperity gospel that promises wealth and success rather than calling believers to a life of surrender and discipleship.

Others promote universalism, denying the exclusivity of Christ's salvation and suggesting that all paths lead to God. Still, others dilute the Gospel, omitting the necessity of a regenerated spirit and the lordship of Jesus Christ in favour of an easy-believism that does not demand transformation.

Deception through cultural compromise

Another way we see deception seeping into the church is through cultural compromise. Instead of standing firm on biblical truth, many Christians conform to the changing moral standards of the world, despite this warning:

> **Romans 12:2** *"Do not conform to the pattern of this world, but be transformed by the renewing of your mind. Then you will be able to test and approve what God's will is - his good, pleasing and perfect will."*

In the name of 'inclusivity' and 'tolerance,' some churches have abandoned biblical teaching on sin, marriage, and holiness. The pressure to be accepted by our society has led many to water down the message of the cross, making it more palatable but far less powerful.

When the church begins to echo the culture rather than challenge it, it loses its prophetic voice and its ability to be the salt and light that Jesus commanded it to be.

Deception through spiritual superficiality

In our present age of instant gratification, many Christians are deceived into thinking that a shallow, surface-level faith is sufficient.

Instead of pursuing deep, personal intimacy with God in Christ, they settle for feel-good messages and an emotional experience that lacks any real substance.

Hosea 4:6 *"My people are destroyed from lack of knowledge."*

This superficial approach to faith is clearly evident in a lack of biblical literacy. Many professing believers do not read or study the Word of God, making them easy targets for deception. Remember Jesus' warning:

Matthew 24:24 *"For false messiahs and false prophets will appear and perform great signs and wonders to deceive, if possible, even the elect."*

Without a firm foundation in Scripture, even those with sincere hearts can be led astray.

Deception through emotional manipulation

Many churches have now adopted an entertainment-driven approach to worship and ministry. Sadly, emotionalism has replaced genuine spiritual growth, and people judge their faith experience by how it makes them feel rather than by the truth it imparts. We have forgotten Jeremiah's warning:

Jeremiah 17:9 *"The heart is deceitful above all things and beyond cure. Who can understand it?"*

Some preachers exploit emotions to manipulate people into decisions that are not rooted in conviction. Worship services focus more on producing an emotional high than on leading people towards surrender and personal transformation. While our emotions are a gift from God, they must never override the authority of His Word.

Deception through false unity

Another form of deception in the Church today is the false idea that unity must come at the expense of truth. While Jesus prayed for His followers to be one (John 17:21), He also made it clear that unity must be built on God's Word.

There is now a growing movement across the church that seeks to unite all faiths and denominations under the banner of love and acceptance, often at the cost of biblical integrity. This false unity downplays essential doctrines, such as the deity of Christ, the necessity of the cross, and the authority of Scripture.

Deception through materialism and worldly success

Many Christians have been deceived into believing that material wealth and worldly success are the markers of God's blessing. However, Jesus gave us a clear warning many years ago:

> **Luke 12:15** *"Watch out! Be on your guard against all kinds of greed; life does not consist in an abundance of possessions."*

The church in many places has now embraced a consumer mentality, where people come to God expecting Him to meet their desires rather than surrendering their lives in worship. This mindset always leads us to discontentment, entitlement, and a shallow faith that collapses in times of trial. Genuine riches are found in Christ alone, not in the fleeting treasures of this world (Matthew 6:19-21).

One of the most prevalent forms of deception in modern Christianity is the prosperity gospel - the idea that God's primary desire is for His people to be wealthy, healthy, and successful in worldly terms. This teaching distorts the true Gospel of Jesus Christ, which calls believers to take up their cross and follow Him (Luke 9:23).

Churches that embrace this doctrine often reduce faith to a transactional formula: sow financial seeds to reap abundant blessings.

While God certainly blesses His people, the prosperity gospel has left many disillusioned when their lives do not match the lavish promises of preachers who manipulate emotions for financial gain.

In some cases, entire congregations have been left totally devastated when their leaders have been exposed for financial misconduct.

The downfall of high-profile prosperity preachers has left behind broken trust, spiritual confusion, and even financial ruin for those who gave everything expecting supernatural returns. Meanwhile, the biblical call to godliness and contentment in Christ (1 Tim. 6:6-10) is seriously neglected.

Spiritual manipulation and cult-like leadership

Deception also manifests in spiritual manipulation, where certain leaders elevate themselves to an almost divine status, demanding absolute loyalty from their followers.

Under the guise of spiritual authority, they silence dissent, twist Scripture for personal gain, and create environments of fear rather than faith.

History is replete with stories of churches and ministries that began with good intentions but spiralled into control, abuse, and scandal.

Whether it is through authoritarian leadership, legalism, or outright heresy, such environments breed deception and lead to deep spiritual wounds.

Tragically, many who have been harmed by such deception walk away not just from corrupt leaders but from the whole church and the Christian faith.

The cost of silence and compromise

One of the greatest tragedies of deception in the church is the cost of silence and compromise. When biblical truth is diluted just to avoid controversy or to seek favour with the world, the church loses its saltiness (Matthew 5:13). Many Christians, though recognising falsehood, remain silent out of the fear of offending others, losing friendships, or facing societal backlash.

History has shown that whenever the church fails to stand against deception, it suffers. Consider the churches that remained silent during historical injustices, refusing to speak out against oppression or immorality.

Today, many churches are facing the same test: will they stand for truth, or will they succumb to the pressures of the culture?

Standing firm against deception

In a world filled with deception, the church must return to the unshakable foundation of God's Word. Paul exhorts us in Ephesians 6:14 to, "*Stand firm then, with the belt of truth buckled around your waist.*"

To guard against deception, believers must:

- **Know the Truth**: A deep and personal knowledge of Scripture is our best defence against the lies which come against us (2 Timothy 2:15).
- **Discern by the Spirit**: The Holy Spirit guides us into all truth (John 16:13) and gives us wisdom to discern falsehood.
- **Be rooted in Christ**: Our faith must be always be built on Christ alone, rather than emotions, trends, or popular opinion (Colossians 2:6-8).

- **Test everything**: We must test all teaching against the truth of Scripture (1 Thessalonians 5:21).

Deception is a powerful tool of the enemy, but those who stand firm in the truth of God's Word will not be led astray. Hear the words of Jesus again:

> **John 8:31-32** *"If you hold to my teaching, you are really my disciples. Then you will know the truth, and the truth will set you free."*

The church must always remain vigilant, unwavering, and committed to proclaiming the unchanging Gospel of Jesus Christ, no matter how the world shifts around us.

Jesus promised that the gates of hell would not prevail against His church (Matthew 16:18). While deception may seek to infiltrate and destroy, the truth of the Gospel remains unshaken. Those who stand firm in Christ will not be swayed by the shifting tides of culture but will shine as beacons of truth in a dark world. As we rise above this crisis, let us remember the words of Paul:

> **1 Corinthians 15:58** *"Therefore, my dear brothers and sisters, stand firm. Let nothing move you. Always give yourselves fully to the work of the Lord, because you know that your labour in the Lord is not in vain."*

6. DISBELIEF

The story of Abraham begins in Genesis 11. We are told that Abraham received, by grace, through faith a whole new life through a child born to him in his old age. In Romans 4, it says he inherited the earth by believing God. Along with his believing, Abraham acted on his belief. He didn't work to obtain, earn or create God's promise of a child, but he worked with God in receiving it. He would never have received the promise otherwise.

Abraham acted in faith in accordance with the promise God had given him, being fully persuaded that God had power needed to do exactly what He promised. (Romans 4:19-20). Abraham acted as if the Word of God was true. He believed God and acted accordingly! Another great story is found in 2 Kings 5:1-14, it tells us about Naaman.

> *"Now Naaman was the Commander of the army of the king of Aram. He was a great man in the sight of his master and highly regarded, because through him the Lord had given victory to Aram. He was a valiant soldier, but he had leprosy. Now bands from Aram had gone out and had taken captive a young girl from Israel, and she served Naaman's wife. She said to her mistress,*
>
> *'If only my master would see the prophet who is in Samaria! He would cure him of his leprosy.' Naaman went to his master, and told him what the girl from Israel had said. 'By all means, go,' the king of Aram replied. 'I will send a letter to the king of Israel.'*
>
> *"So Naaman left, taking with him ten talents of silver, six thousand shekels of gold and ten sets of clothing.*

The letter he took to the king of Israel read: With this letter I am sending my servant Naaman to you so that you may cure him of his leprosy.' As soon as the king of Israel read the letter, he tore his robes and said, 'Am I God? Can I kill and bring back to life? Why does this fellow send someone to me to be cured of his leprosy? See how he is trying to pick a quarrel with me!

When Elisha the man of God heard that the king of Israel had torn his robes, he sent him this message: 'Why have you torn your robes? Have the man come to me and he will know that there is a prophet in Israel.' So Naaman went with his horses and chariots and stopped at the door of Elisha's house."

When Naaman arrives at Elisha's house, with his robes, chariots and in great pomp, the prophet of God doesn't even come out of the house! He's out the back, fixing the washing machine!

"Elisha sent a messenger to say to him, 'Go, wash yourself seven times in the Jordan, and your flesh will be restored and you will be cleansed.' But Naaman went away angry and said, 'I thought that he would surely come out to me and stand and call on the name of the Lord his God, wave his hand over the spot and cure me of my leprosy.' (he was expecting something religious or magical). Are not the Abana and Pharpar, the rivers in Damascus, better than any of the waters of Israel? Couldn't I wash in them and be cleansed?' So he turned and went off in a rage.

Naaman's servants went to him and said, 'My father, if the prophet had told you to do some great thing, would you not have done it? How much more, then, when he tells you, 'Wash and be cleansed!' So he went down and dipped himself in the Jordan seven times, as the man of God had told him, and his flesh was restored and became clean like that of a young boy."

The Word of God to Naaman was clear, through Elisha. He was effectively given healing by the grace of God through Elisha's command to wash in the Jordan seven times.

Naaman could act on that and receive the healing from God – or he could ignore it and eventually die from leprosy. The Word of God was true, but he would never have experienced it unless he acted as though it was true. The irritating thing for Naaman (and every religious person that followed him!) is that it just sounded too simple!

We face the same problem today. We can fall into the trap of waiting for some flashy, miraculous sudden intervention from God to solve our problems and make us believe Him – that one thing that is suddenly going to make life work - the conference, book, preacher or experience that will fix us and unlock the blessings and reality of God.

What God gives us is so simple that we often miss it. That's why Jesus said we must come as little children, with the same child-like faith. We receive the free gifts and blessings of God by believing that they are free and then acting on that belief.

> **2 Kings 5:15-16** *"Then Naaman and all his attendants went back to the man of God. He stood before him and said, 'Now I know that there is no God in all the world except in Israel. Please now accept a gift from your servant.' The prophet answered, 'As surely as the Lord lives, whom I serve, I will not accept a thing.' And even though Naaman urged him, he refused."*

Naaman tried to pay for something that was free. As understandable as that is for humans like us, it's an insult to God who gives freely in love. How would a parent feel if a young child started giving their pocket money back in payment after each meal?

It must break God's heart when His children try to pay Him back for His love and empowering grace. The Apostle Paul tells his own story:

1 Corinthians 15:9-10 *"For I am the least of the apostles and do not even deserve to be called an apostle, (I don't deserve anything I have.) because I persecuted the church of God. But by the grace of God I am what I am, (and I say what I say, and do what I do, and write what I write) and his grace to me was not without effect. No, I worked harder than all of them – yet not I, but the grace of God that was with me."*

Paul clearly says he didn't deserve it, it came to him freely. He got what everyone else in the kingdom got. But it didn't come to him without effect because he worked harder than everybody else. He worked in response to the resources of God's grace. He could have received God's grace and not worked hard and the gift would have been without effect. Abraham could have waited forever if he hadn't acted upon God's word. Naaman could have died in his pride and disease had he not acted.

You may believe in God's free, radical grace. You may affirm that you can never deserve it or earn it or pay it back - but if you don't act as though that is true you will never experience the liberating power of that free gift! It will have no effect.

Jesus explained it to his disciples in Luke 8, with the parable of the seed and the four types of soil. The seed is the Word of God. It comes to you by reading the Bible, listening to sermons, discussion in a small group and directly to your spirit sometimes. The seed always remains the same, but the different soils determine whether the seed will germinate and grow. The good seed sometimes falls on the path. The soil is hard, the seed cannot take root there so it blows away or is snatched by a bird.

Other seed falls on shallow soil and it can't grow there either. It may fall in good soil, but weeds grow up faster and choke the seed to death. But the same seed which fails to grow in those places produces a bountiful crop in fertile soil which is rich, receptive and prepared. The power isn't in the soil, the power is in the seed; but the life and fruit within the seed will never produce its crop without the resources of the soil.

We should spend as much time as we can in the Bible, not for any religious reason to please God, or because it's a discipline we've developed, but because it contains the seed - life-changing, mind-blowing Word of God Almighty, which will produce life in you. If you read it and allow it to penetrate your heart and take root, you will find everything God has promised begin to manifest in your life and that great old hymn written over 100 years ago by Barney Warren will be your testimony. You should look it up and read the words! It's called *Joy unspeakable and full of glory!*

Does that sound like your life? That's the promise of God which will become a reality in your life as you provide the best environment for His Word of truth. First believe it - then start acting as though it's true and you will receive all the fruit God desires. Seeds don't come up overnight, and babies don't arrive the next week. Sometimes there is a time delay as the fruit forms in a hidden place, but the promise will be delivered.

All those great promises of God will in time become your experience: *"I will keep you in perfect peace ... You will be able to do all things through Christ who strengthens you ... Ask anything in my name and I will do it for you."* etc. The Word of God will produce fruit, because it has within it the power to fulfil His promises. All it needs is fertile, deep, rich, open, co-operative soil.

It's never a case of God's part then our part following, we do it together all the way - or it doesn't happen. The Bible and our own experiences confirm that the first sin that nullifies the promises, power and manifest presence of God in our experience, but not in reality, is the sin of unbelief.

Ephesians 1:3 *"Praise be to the God and Father of our Lord Jesus Christ, who has blessed us in the heavenly realms with every spiritual blessing in Christ."*

If you are a believer, you now have everything in Christ, but if you don't act on that belief you will never experience it. The next verse tells us the most important blessing of all:

Ephesians 1:4 *"For he chose us in him before the creation of the world to be holy and blameless in his sight."*

He has already done all that. Any attempt on our part to become holy in His sight in sin, and we need to repent of that sin of unbelief. Unbelief gives rise to every other sin in life, from the Garden of Eden till now.

Why do believers still covet, steal, commit adultery or lie? It's because they don't believe they already have everything in Christ. You don't need to strive for acceptance in Christ; you don't need to attain God's holiness by your religious performance; you don't need drugs to find peace with God; you never need to try and manipulate people into liking you, because you are loved by God. Just believe it!

Unbelief is the first sin. All other sin that we feel bad about is our futile attempt to earn the things that God has already freely given us. God said to Adam and Eve: *"I give you everything in abundance. It is all good."* Then the serpent said, *"God is withholding something from you. If you really want to live, then in addition to all that God has given you, you need to take this forbidden fruit."*

Taking the fruit was not Adam and Eve's first sin. Not believing what God had told them was their first sin.

> **Ephesians 1:5-6** *"In love he predestined us to be adopted as his sons and daughters through Jesus Christ, in accordance with his pleasure and will – to the praise of his glorious grace, which he has freely given us in the One he loves."*

There is no more that we need. We just need to believe what we are told and step out and act as if it were true. That's faith. We have ALL we need for life in Jesus Christ; ALL we need for godliness; ALL we need for happiness; ALL we need for authentic life; ALL we need for our church to look like the church Christ intended.

If we have prepared good, rich, open and receptive soil, meditate on the fact that we have everything in Christ and act as if that fact were true, we will begin to experience what the Word promises to us. If we don't, we won't – it's that simple.

Our lives are full of all kinds of sins, and we tend to put them in different categories, and we repent of them as we feel convicted, but until we repent of the first sin of unbelief, our lives will never work, and we will go on committing many other sins which flow from unbelief.

God told Abraham that he and Sarah would have a son. Abraham's unbelief caused him to try to help out by having a son with Hagar. He then had to repent of his second sin as well as the sin of unbelief. I have endeavoured in many ways to demonstrate your complete freedom in Christ; that you are ok with God; and that His life is given to you freely, and you never have to earn it. Why have I done that? Why has this seemed like a cracked record? There are a number of reasons:

Firstly, it's New Testament truth, and we all need to hear it often. Secondly, as brothers and sisters in Christ, I want you to become increasingly more free, full of joy and confidence, experiencing more and more of the abundant life which is yours in Christ.

The third reason is that if you really believe and act on what I have been telling you, sin will not be an issue. Paul tells us in Romans 6 that we are no longer slaves to sin. Hebrews 10 tells us that we have been made holy and presented to God, perfect in Christ. Then there's this:

> **Romans 4:13-16** *"It was not through law that Abraham and his offspring received the promise that he would be heir of the world, but through the righteousness that comes by faith. For if those who live by law are heirs, faith has no value and the promise is worthless, because law brings wrath. And where there is no law there is no transgression. Therefore, the promise comes by faith, so that it may be by grace."*

The promise comes by faith so that it may be in accordance with grace. Grace means you don't have to work for it – you get it free. If it's by faith, anyone can do it.

Religion says: *'You reach God's highest purposes if you are a good pray-er. You need to live a life of holiness and purity to reach spiritual maturity. You will only stand in the end-times army of God if you clean up your act.'*

No, no, no!! You get it by faith, by believing what you've been told and acting on that, according to grace.

Anybody can believe, you don't need super intelligence, you don't need the right connections, you don't need to be wealthy or good-looking. You just need to believe!

Jesus' disciples asked Him: *"What must we do to do the works of God?"* (John 6:28,29) Jesus told them: *"This is the work of God – to believe in the One He sent."* This is our primary work – to believe in Jesus. If you want to work hard for God, let that belief be translated into action: become the person you already are in Christ.

Belief without action is not belief at all. Abraham believed God's promise to him, and a son was born. Naaman washed himself in a muddy river and his skin was healed.

The Apostle Paul expressed his incredible view of God's liberating and all-encompassing grace as he travelled the world preaching and establishing the church, and writing his teaching down which has now been preserved for us. All three men were given promises which would never have borne fruit if they hadn't participated with God by faith and believed.

That is why it is so crucial that we understand the full implications of God's grace, and all we have in Christ. We need to know deep in our hearts that we are OK because Jesus made us OK, and therefore, Jesus plus nothing is our salvation and our life.

That is the only solid foundation for building the Church. God will remove any other, because anything built on a wrong foundation cannot last.

In the final analysis, if our life is not working, if we are struggling, hurting, suffering physically, emotionally or spiritually, it's not because of our mother or father or anyone else's sin against us – past, present or future – it's not even ultimately because of the secondary sins in our own life. All of our main problems actually arise from the primary sin of unbelief.

When we know that we are totally, unconditionally loved, accepted and made holy before God and empowered by His free grace as given in Christ, we are no longer intimidated by anything, either from without or within – even our own sins and shortcomings. We can hand them over to God once and for all.

The Bible is the account of men and women's experiences with God. It is His story, rather than ours. God is the central character – Creator, Author, Hero and Finisher of this long narrative, and as the story unfolds, so does the revelation about Him.

From the beginning, He is a God of grace, choosing people and making promises to them, blessing them, and keeping His promises despite their failure. Such is His love that He always treats His people with dignity and respect, allowing them to respond to Him by their own choice.

Those commended by God in Hebrews 11 are the ones who chose to believe His word, take part in His plans, and see the fruit emerge in their lives.

> **Hebrews 12:1-3** *"Therefore, since we are surrounded by such a great cloud of witnesses, let us throw off everything that hinders and the sin that so easily entangles, and let us run with perseverance the race marked out for us.*
>
> *Let us fix our eyes on Jesus, the author and perfector of our faith, who for the joy set before him endured the cross, scorning its shame, and sat down at the right hand of the throne of God. Consider him who endured such opposition from sinful men, so that you will not grow weary and lose heart."*

7. DISCONNECTION

The modern church faces a crisis of disconnection - both from one another and, more tragically, from God. The early church was characterized by deep, meaningful fellowship, a shared sense of purpose, and a constant connection to the presence of God. However, in today's individualistic, fast-paced, and digital-driven world, many believers have grown increasingly isolated.

The biblical vision of the church as a united body of Christ has been weakened today by superficial relationships, self-centred faith, and a lack of true spiritual intimacy. The consequences are profound, leading to increased spiritual apathy, disillusionment, and a weakening of our collective witness to the world.

One of the most defining characteristics of the early Church was its strong sense of community. Acts 2:42 describes it vividly: *"They devoted themselves to the apostles' teaching and to fellowship, to the breaking of bread and to prayer."* This deep connection - referred to in the Greek as *koinonia* - was more than just casual social interaction; it was a committed, sacrificial, and spiritually enriching relationship.

Yet, in many churches today, this sense of true community has been lost. Instead of vibrant, life-giving relationships, many believers attend church as passive spectators rather than active participants in a spiritual family. Small talk and surface-level interactions have replaced genuine concern, accountability, and sacrificial love for one another.

The Importance of 'One Another' in Scripture

The New Testament repeatedly emphasizes the need for believers to care for, support, and love one another.

The phrase "*one another*" appears over 50 times, reinforcing the idea that Christianity is not a solitary faith but a shared journey. Consider just a few of these directives:

Love one another - *A new command I give you: Love one another. As I have loved you, so you must love one another. By this everyone will know that you are my disciples."*

(John 13:34-35)

Encourage one another *"Therefore encourage one another and build each other up, just as in fact you are doing."*

(1 Thessalonians 5:11)

Bear one another's burdens *"Carry each other's burdens, and in this way you will fulfill the law of Christ."*

(Galatians 6:2)

Forgive one another *"Bear with each other and forgive one another if any of you has a grievance against someone. Forgive as the Lord forgave you."* (Colossians 3:13)

These verses paint a picture of a Church community that is interconnected, supportive, and deeply invested in each other's lives. However, the increasing individualism in society has crept into the church, leading many to prioritize personal comfort over communal responsibility.

The Digital Church: A Blessing and a Curse

While technology has allowed the Gospel to reach more people than ever before, it has also contributed to the problem of disconnection. Many now experience church solely through online sermons, missing out on the vital aspects of fellowship, accountability, and service. The bible warns against this trend.

Hebrews 10:24-25 *"And let us consider how we may spur one another on toward love and good deeds, not giving up meeting together, as some are in the habit of doing, but encouraging one another - and all the more as you see the Day approaching."*

Virtual church can be a supplement but never a substitute for the embodied experience of gathering with fellow believers. A screen cannot replace a hug from a brother or sister in Christ, the laying on of hands in prayer, or the warmth of communal worship.

When believers disconnect from in-person fellowship, they risk spiritual stagnation and loneliness, making them more vulnerable to the enemy's attacks.

Even more concerning than our disconnection from one another is our disconnection from God Himself. Many believers go through the motions of faith - attending church, reading devotionals, and even praying - without actually abiding in Christ. Jesus warns about this danger:

John 15:5 *"I am the vine; you are the branches. If you remain in me and I in you, you will bear much fruit; apart from me you can do nothing."*

The symptoms of spiritual disconnection

Prayerlessness: Many Christians find themselves too busy or distracted to spend time in prayer, reducing their relationship with God to a mere intellectual belief rather than a vital daily walk of intimacy.

In 1 Thessalonians 5:17 Paul urges us to *"pray continually,"* emphasizing the need for ongoing communion with God.

Biblical illiteracy: Fewer believers are deeply engaging with Scripture, leading to a faith built on opinions rather than truth. Psalm 119:105 declares, *"Your word is a lamp for my feet, a light on my path."* Without this guiding light, many stumble into confusion and compromise.

Spiritual apathy: A heart disconnected from God becomes indifferent to spiritual matters. Jesus rebuked the church in Laodicea for their lukewarm faith in Revelation 3:16: *"So, because you are lukewarm - neither hot nor cold - I am about to spit you out of my mouth."*

Moral compromise: When believers drift from God, they are more susceptible to temptation and sin. James 4:8 gives the solution: *"Come near to God and he will come near to you. Wash your hands, you sinners, and purify your hearts, you double-minded."*

How do we reconnect?

Restoring our connection to God and one another is not just an option - it is a necessity for the Church to overcome this crisis and thrive again. The solution lies in returning to the biblical model of faith, where community and intimacy with God are prioritized above all else.

Return to authentic fellowship: Churches must cultivate environments where believers genuinely share life together, not just attend services and meetings. Prioritizing small groups, accountability partnerships, and a variety of service opportunities is the only way back to authentic fellowship.

Commit to deep prayer and worship: Revival begins in the prayer closet. Believers must reestablish a consistent, fervent prayer life and engage in worship that seeks the presence of God rather than entertainment.

Engage with Scripture daily: The Bible must once again become central in our lives. Psalm 1:2-3 says, *"But whose delight is in the law of the Lord, and who meditates on his law day and night. That person is like a tree planted by streams of water."*

Prioritize fellowship: Whether in small groups or in corporate worship, believers must make gathering with other Christians a non-negotiable commitment in their spiritual lives.

Seek the power of the Holy Spirit – True reconnection comes through the Spirit of God, who empowers us to walk in love, truth, and unity (Ephesians 4:3).

The crisis of disconnection is really one of the most serious challenges facing the contemporary church. When we are disconnected from one another, we fail to reflect the body of Christ. When we are disconnected from God, we drift into spiritual emptiness. But there is hope.

The call to return to biblical community and deep intimacy with the Lord is ever-present. As we reconnect with God and with each other, we will once again become the powerful, unified, and Spirit-filled church that Jesus birthed and promised to build.

8. DECENSION / DIVISION

The Christian church, called to be the body of Christ and a beacon of unity, is increasingly plagued by division and dissension. When Jesus walked among us, He prayed for the unity of His followers, saying, *"that all of them may be one, Father, just as you are in me and I am in you."* (John 17:21).

Yet, modern Christianity is rife with theological disputes, denominational splits, and political conflicts that threaten to undermine its witness to the world. This chapter will seek to examine the causes, consequences, and biblical solutions to the crisis of division within the church.

The root causes of division

Doctrinal disputes

One of the most persistent causes of division in the church is doctrinal disagreement. From debates over salvation and sacraments to varying interpretations of biblical prophecy, theological differences have led to countless schisms. While doctrine is always important, Paul warns against fruitless arguments:

> **2 Timothy 2:14** *"Remind them of this, and warn them before God[a] that they are to avoid wrangling over words, which does no good but only ruins those who are listening."*

Unfortunately, rather than fostering constructive dialogue, many disputes have led to permanent fractures within the body of Christ. The early church also dealt with doctrinal disagreements, particularly regarding the relationship between Jewish and Gentile believers. Paul and the apostles had to settle disputes over circumcision, dietary laws, and other religious practices (Acts 15:1-29).

Their resolution demonstrated a balance between holding to essential truths while allowing for differences in non-essential matters. This biblical example serves as a guide for contemporary Christians who must daily navigate doctrinal differences with wisdom and grace.

Denominational fragmentation

The Christian church has fragmented into thousands of denominations (48,000 at last count!), each one with distinct theological and liturgical practices. While diversity can be healthy, division that leads to hostility and exclusion is a clear contradiction of the biblical mandate for unity. That's why Paul admonished the Corinthians:

> **1 Corinthians 1:10** *"Now I appeal to you, brothers and sisters, by the name of our Lord Jesus Christ, that all of you should be in agreement and that there should be no divisions among you, but that you should be united in the same mind and the same purpose."*

Denominational splits often stem from differing views on issues such as baptism, church governance, or spiritual gifts. While some divisions have been necessary to preserve biblical integrity, many have occurred due to personal disagreements, cultural influences, or misinterpretations of Scripture. Instead of working through the conflicts with humility and grace, many believers choose to separate, weakening the collective witness of the church.

Cultural and political influences

In many churches, cultural and political affiliations have taken precedence over the gospel, creating rifts among believers. Political divisions have led to conflicts where congregants find themselves more aligned with secular ideologies than with their brothers and sisters in Christ.

Yet Scripture reminds us that our primary allegiance is always to the Kingdom of God:

Philippians 3:20 *"But our citizenship is in heaven, and it is from there that we are expecting a Saviour, the Lord Jesus Christ.*

The early church faced similar challenges, as Jewish and Gentile believers tried to merge two vastly different cultural backgrounds. Paul encouraged the church to embrace unity in Christ rather than allowing cultural differences to create hostility (Ephesians 2:14-16).

Today, churches must ensure that their primary identity is rooted in Christ, rather than in political parties or national affiliations.

Personal conflicts and pride

Much division within local churches stems from personal disputes and a lack of humility. Leaders and members sometimes allow pride and ego to drive their interactions, causing unnecessary strife. James addresses this issue:

James 4:1 *"What causes fights and quarrels among you? Don't they come from your desires that battle within you?"*

Leadership issues, personal grudges, and competition for influence can lead to conflicts in the church that distract from the mission of Christ.

Paul warned against such behaviour, urging believers to *"be completely humble and gentle; be patient, bearing with one another in love"* (Ephesians 4:2). Humility and a commitment to reconciliation are essential to overcoming personal disputes in the church.

The Consequences of Division

Weakening of the church's witness

Jesus declared that unity among believers would be a testimony to the world: *"By this everyone will know that you are my disciples, if you love one another."* (John 13:35). A divided church loses its credibility and effectiveness in spreading the gospel.

Non-believers often view Christian disunity as hypocrisy, questioning how a faith built on love and grace can be so fragmented. When churches seem to prioritize division over reconciliation, they significantly hinder the mission of Christ to reach the lost.

Spiritual stagnation and decline

When believers focus more on disputes than discipleship, the church suffers spiritually. Instead of growing in faith, many churches become stagnant or experience decline, as members become disillusioned and leave.

Statistics indicate that younger generations are leaving the church in record numbers. While various factors contribute to this trend, internal division and a lack of unity within the church play a significant role. A church that models Christ-like love and unity will be far more effective in engaging future generations.

Opportunities for the enemy to exploit

Division creates vulnerabilities that Satan can exploit. Jesus warned, *"If a house is divided against itself, that house cannot stand"* (Mark 3:25). The church, when fractured, becomes susceptible to false teachings, moral compromise, and external persecution.

Biblical Solutions for Unity

Focusing on Christ as the centre

True unity is only found in Christ. Paul emphasizes this:

> **Ephesians 4:4-6** *"There is one body and one Spirit, just as you were called to one hope when you were called; one Lord, one faith, one baptism; one God and Father of all, who is over all and through all and in all."*

Practicing humility and love

Humility allows Christians to put aside all their personal preferences and work together in love. Paul encourages believers:

> **Philippians 2:3** *"Do nothing from selfish ambition or conceit, but in humility regard others as better than yourselves."*

Pursuing reconciliation and forgiveness

The Church must be a model of reconciliation. It requires effort, but it reflects the heart of the gospel.

> **Matthew 5:9** *"Blessed are the peacemakers, for they will be called children of God."*

Holding fast to Biblical truth while avoiding legalism

Paul warns against legalism, saying, *"For the letter kills, but the Spirit gives life"* (2 Corinthians 3:6). Churches must stand firm on core biblical truths while allowing for grace in secondary matters.

Committing to Prayer and the Work of the Holy Spirit

Through prayer and surrender to the Spirit, the church can experience true oneness.

Ephesians 4:3 *"Make every effort to keep the unity of the Spirit through the bond of peace."*

The crisis of dissention and division in the Church is really serious, but it's not insurmountable. As believers commit to focusing on Christ; remaining humble; always pursuing reconciliation; standing firm on truth without legalism; and seeking the Holy Spirit's guidance, the church can move toward the true unity Jesus desires.

May we remember His prayer and strive to live as one body, reflecting His love and truth to the world.

9. DISILLUSIONMENT

One of the most pervasive crises facing the modern Church is the growing sense of disillusionment among believers. Disillusionment occurs when expectations are unmet, when faith is shaken, and when individuals begin to question the authenticity of their beliefs, their leaders, and even God Himself.

This phenomenon has led many to disengage from the Church, retreat into spiritual apathy, or abandon the faith altogether. In a time when the world is more divided than ever, the church must confront this issue head-on, and recognise its causes, its consequences, and the biblical path toward restoration.

The causes of disillusionment

Disillusionment in the church can stem from a number of sources, both internal and external. While some factors are unique to individuals, others are systemic issues that have plagued the Church for generations.

The failure of Christian leaders

One of the most significant contributors to disillusionment is the moral and ethical failure of Christian leaders. High-profile scandals, financial corruption, and abuse within church leadership have deeply wounded many believers. When those entrusted with shepherding God's people fall into sin, the result is often a crisis of faith for their followers.

Jesus warned against false shepherds in John 10:12-13. "*The hired hand is not the shepherd and does not own the sheep. So when he sees the wolf coming, he abandons the sheep and runs away. Then the wolf attacks the flock and scatters it. The man runs away because he is a hired hand and cares nothing for the sheep.*"

Many believers have experienced the pain of being abandoned or deceived by leaders who prioritize power and prestige over humility and service. When leadership fails, the faith of many is shaken.

The Hypocrisy of the church

Another major cause of disillusionment is the disconnect between what the Church preaches and what it practices. When believers witness judgmental attitudes, gossip, division, and a lack of love within the Church, they begin to question the authenticity of the Christian message.

Jesus rebuked the Pharisees for their hypocrisy:

> **Matthew 23:27** *"Woe to you, teachers of the law and Pharisees, you hypocrites! You are like whitewashed tombs, which look beautiful on the outside but on the inside are full of the bones of the dead and everything unclean."*

When churches fail to embody the grace, love, and humility of Christ, disillusionment takes root, leading many to walk away from the faith.

The prosperity gospel and false expectations

A distorted gospel message has also played a significant role in disillusionment. The prosperity gospel, which teaches that faith guarantees wealth and success, has set many believers up for disappointment. When suffering and hardship inevitably come, those who have been led to believe that faith should shield them from all trials begin to question their beliefs. Jesus never promised an easy life; in fact, He said the opposite here:

> **John 16:33** *"In this world you will have trouble. But take heart! I have overcome the world."*

When churches promote a gospel that is more about personal gain than sacrificial love, they create expectations that will ultimately lead to disappointment.

Church division and political entanglement

The increasing politicization of the church has certainly contributed to widespread disillusionment. Many believers feel alienated when churches align themselves too closely with political ideologies, creating divisions rather than unity.

The church was never meant to be an extension of any political party; its allegiance is to Christ alone. Paul warns against division.

> **1 Corinthians 1:10** *"I appeal to you, brothers and sisters, in the name of our Lord Jesus Christ, that all of you agree with one another in what you say and that there be no divisions among you, but that you be perfectly united in mind and thought."*

When the church becomes more focused on many worldly agendas than the Kingdom of God, it loses credibility and drives many believers away.

The consequences of disillusionment

When disillusionment sets in, the results can be devastating. It often leads to isolation, spiritual apathy, and even a complete departure from the faith.

Apathy and withdrawal from church community

Many disillusioned believers choose to withdraw from the church entirely, opting to live a private faith without the support and accountability of a spiritual community. However, Scripture warns against forsaking fellowship:

Hebrews 10:25 *"Not giving up meeting together, as some are in the habit of doing, but encouraging one another - and all the more as you see the Day approaching."*

Separation from the body of Christ leads to spiritual stagnation, making believers more susceptible to doubt and despair.

Cynicism and a hardening of the heart

Disillusionment often breeds cynicism, making it difficult for believers to trust church leadership, fellow Christians, or even God. When faith becomes tainted by scepticism, it weakens our ability to experience the joy and power of a transformed life.

Proverbs 4:23 *"Above all else, guard your heart, for everything you do flows from it."*

A hardened heart can make it nearly impossible to receive the truth and love of God, leading many into spiritual decay.

Turning away from faith

Perhaps the most tragic consequence of disillusionment is when believers abandon the faith altogether. Many who once followed Christ with passion have renounced their beliefs because of hurt, disappointment, or doubt.

2 Timothy 4:10 *"For Demas, because he loved this world, has deserted me and has gone to Thessalonica."*

When disillusionment is not addressed, it can lead to a slow but steady departure from God's truth. When that happens, people lose the ability to discern anything from God and can quickly become disillusioned.

Overcoming disillusionment

Disillusionment does not have to be the end of faith. Instead, it can be a catalyst for a deeper, more mature relationship with God.

Fixing our eyes on Jesus, not people

While human leaders will fail, Christ never will. The write of Hebrews encourages us here: *"Fixing our eyes on Jesus, the pioneer and perfecter of faith."* (Hebrews 12:2)

When we build our faith on Christ rather than flawed individuals, we quickly develop a faith that is resilient and enduring.

Embracing biblical truth, not cultural Christianity

Returning to the unchanging truth of Scripture helps believers distinguish between genuine faith and man-made distortions of the Gospel.

Psalm 119:160 *"All your words are true; all your righteous laws are eternal."*

The Bible, not tradition or personal preferences, must be our foundation.

Committing to authentic Christian community

Instead of withdrawing from the church, believers should seek out authentic, Spirit-filled communities where faith is lived out with humility and love. Healing comes through genuine relationships with fellow believers. We are created to be in community together – mutually dependent upon each other under God.

Trusting in God's sovereignty

Even when the Church fails, God's plan remains unshaken.

> **Romans 8:28** *"And we know that in all things God works for the good of those who love him, who have been called according to his purpose."*

Trusting in God's sovereignty allows believers to persevere through disappointment and find hope beyond the failures of man.

Disillusionment is a real and painful experience, but it does not have to lead to destruction. By refocusing on Christ, embracing biblical truth, and committing to authentic community, believers can overcome disillusionment and emerge with a faith that is stronger than ever.

The church may be imperfect, but God's plan for His people remains perfect. He is still at work, calling His children to walk in truth, love, and steadfast hope.

10. DISEMPOWERMENT

The church of Jesus Christ was never meant to function in human strength alone. From its very inception at Pentecost, the church was birthed in the power of the Holy Spirit. Jesus Himself commanded His disciples to wait until they were *"clothed with power from on high."* (Luke 24:49).

Tragically, in modern times, many believers and even entire congregations attempt to carry out the work of God in their own strength, intellect, and ability.

The result is spiritual exhaustion, ineffective ministry, and a church that lacks the supernatural power it was designed to manifest. This crisis of disempowerment has left many Christians frustrated, weary, and fruitless.

The necessity of the Holy Spirit's power

Jesus made it abundantly clear that His followers could not fulfill their mission apart from divine empowerment.

> **Acts 1:8** *"But you will receive power when the Holy Spirit comes on you; and you will be my witnesses in Jerusalem, and in all Judea and Samaria, and to the ends of the earth."*

Without this power, the disciples would have been ill-equipped to carry out the Great Commission. The early Church understood this dependency on the Holy Spirit.

> **Acts 4:31** *"After they prayed, the place where they were meeting was shaken. And they were all filled with the Holy Spirit and spoke the word of God boldly."*

The power of God was not an optional enhancement to their ministry - it was the very foundation of it.

However, in today's church, many believers attempt to serve God without the power of the Spirit. They rely on personal skills, theological knowledge, or church programs rather than seeking the anointing of God.

This lack of divine empowerment usually leads to burnout, stagnation, and ineffective witness. Programs soon replace prayer, human effort substitutes for divine intervention, and strategies take precedence over Spirit-led obedience. The result is a church that operates with a form of godliness but denies its power (2 Timothy 3:5).

The folly of ministering in our own strength

Scripture gives several examples of what happens when people try to do God's work apart from His power:

Moses and his impulsiveness: Before being empowered by God, Moses tried to deliver Israel through his own strength by killing an Egyptian (Exodus 2:11-12). This act of self-reliance led to exile rather than deliverance. Only when he encountered God at the burning bush and received divine commissioning did he become the true deliverer of Israel (Exodus 3:12).

Samson's loss of lower: Samson was a man set apart for God's purposes, yet when he compromised with the world, he lost his divine strength. Judges 16:20 records one of the most tragic moments in Scripture: *"But he did not know that the Lord had left him."* Without the Spirit's power, he was just another man - vulnerable, weak, and ineffective.

The disciples' failure before Pentecost: Before the Holy Spirit came upon them, the disciples were fearful and powerless. Peter, who later preached boldly at Pentecost, was the same man who denied Christ three times in fear (Luke 22:61-62).

The difference? The Spirit's empowerment of the Spirit transformed him from a coward to a courageous witness (Acts 2:14-41).

The sons of Sceva: In Acts 19, Jewish exorcists attempted to cast out demons in their own power, using the name of Jesus without a relationship with Him. The result was disastrous - the evil spirit overpowered them, exposing their lack of divine authority. This story is a sobering reminder that spiritual work cannot be accomplished through human strength alone.

These examples serve as warnings for us today. When we attempt to fulfill God's work in our own strength, we will inevitably fall short. Human effort, no matter how sincere, can never replace the necessity of divine empowerment.

Symptoms of a disempowered church

How can we recognize when we or our churches are operating without the power of the Holy Spirit? Here are some signs:

Spiritual burnout: Many Christians feel overwhelmed and exhausted in ministry. Instead of serving with joy and power, they feel drained because they are relying on human effort rather than the Spirit's strength (Zechariah 4:6, NIV: "Not by might nor by power, but by my Spirit, says the Lord Almighty").

Lack of supernatural fruit: Jesus said in John 15:5 (NIV): "Apart from me you can do nothing." A disempowered church may be busy with activities but see little true transformation in people's lives. Without the Spirit, there is no lasting spiritual fruit.

Fear and hesitation: When Christians lack the Holy Spirit's power, they struggle to share their faith boldly. Acts 4:31 clearly shows that the Spirit emboldens believers to witness powerfully.

Dependence on human methods: Instead of seeking God's guidance, many churches turn to marketing strategies, entertainment, or business models to grow. While structure is important, true Kingdom growth only comes through the Spirit's work .

> **1 Corinthians 2:4-5** *"My message and my preaching were not with wise and persuasive words, but with a demonstration of the Spirit's power."*

Absence of spiritual gifts: A church without the power of the Spirit often lacks the manifestation of spiritual gifts. When the Holy Spirit is at work, believers are equipped with gifts such as prophecy, healing, discernment, and faith (1 Corinthians 12:7-11). A church devoid of these expressions is often relying on human effort rather than divine enablement.

The path to re-empowerment

The good news is that we do not have to remain in a state of disempowerment. God desires to fill His people afresh with His Spirit. Here's how we can return to the power of God:

Seek the filling of the Holy Spirit: Jesus instructed His disciples to wait for the Holy Spirit before beginning their ministry (Acts 1:4-5). We, too, must actively seek a fresh infilling of His power (Ephesians 5:18 *"Be filled with the Spirit"*).

Develop a lifestyle of prayer and dependence on God: The early church was a praying church. Before every major move of God, they gathered in unified prayer (Acts 2:42, Acts 4:31). A prayerless church is a powerless church.

Step out in faith and obedience: The Holy Spirit empowers us as we step out in faith. Peter and John healed the lame man at the temple gate through the Spirit's power, not their own ability (Acts 3:6-7).

Walk in holiness and surrender: Sin and compromise quench the Holy Spirit's work (Ephesians 4:30). To walk in power, we must yield fully to God, forsaking anything that hinders His presence.

Desire spiritual gifts and use them: 1 Corinthians 12:7 says, *"Now to each one the manifestation of the Spirit is given for the common good."* God empowers His people with spiritual gifts for the edification of the church and the advancement of the Gospel.

The church was never meant to function in its own strength. We were created by God to be vessels of the Holy Spirit, empowered for Kingdom service. Now is the time to return to Pentecost, to seek the fullness of the Spirit, and to walk in the supernatural power of God.

As Zechariah 4:6 reminds us: *"Not by might nor by power, but by my Spirit, says the Lord Almighty."*

11. DECISION TIME!

The journey through this book has been a sobering one. We have explored the crises that threaten the church in this generation:

Distraction	Deception	Dissension
Discouragement	Disbelief	Disillusionment
Dissatisfaction	Disconnection	Disempowerment

These are not mere theoretical concerns; they are real and present dangers that have weakened believers, crippled congregations and hindered the advance of God's kingdom. However, this book was never meant to simply highlight the problems. The purpose has always been to awaken, equip, and empower God's people to respond in faith, and now, we have arrived at a decisive moment.

Throughout history, every major crisis the church has faced has demanded a response. Some have risen to the challenge, standing firm in truth and pressing forward in faithfulness. Sadly, others have faltered, succumbing to compromise, complacency, or fear. We stand at such a crossroads today.

The question before us is simple: What will we do? Will we retreat in fear, surrendering to the forces that seek to weaken and divide us? Or will we rise up, renewed in our devotion to Christ, committed to His mission, and resolved to live as His victorious disciples?

Allow me to finish this book by identifying the six key priorities facing us as we respond to the crisis facing the church in these difficult times. God has assured us that we have everything we need, in Christ, to stand against all the attacks coming against the church. We just need to decide if we have the will to embrace these challenges.

1. Returning to our first love

At the heart of every spiritual crisis is a misalignment of priorities. The Ephesian church received this warning from Jesus:

> **Revelation 2:4** *"Yet I hold this against you: You have forsaken the love you had at first."*

If we are to overcome the crises that plague the church, we must return to our first love - Jesus Christ. He is not merely a doctrine to be defended or a name to be preached; He is our life, our passion, our whole reason for being. Without an intimate, daily walk with Christ, our faith will always be vulnerable to distraction and deception.

A renewed love for Jesus means far more than emotional fervour. It means prioritizing His Word, spending time in prayer, and allowing the Holy Spirit to transform us. It means that the driving force of our lives is not tradition, personal preference, or worldly success, but Christ alone.

2. Reclaiming biblical truth

In an age of deception and disbelief, the church needs to recommit itself to the absolute authority of Scripture. Paul warned Timothy:

> **2 Timothy 4:3** *"For the time will come when people will not put up with sound doctrine. Instead, to suit their own desires, they will gather around them a great number of teachers to say what their itching ears want to hear."*

We see this playing out in churches today - truth is being diluted, doctrines are being compromised, and cultural trends dictate theology rather than the Word of God.

But we must remember: the Word of God is eternal, unchanging, and sufficient. If we are to stand firm, we must immerse ourselves in Scripture daily, teaching it faithfully, defending it courageously, and living it out. We do not need innovation; we need a return to the gospel's power.

3. Restoring unity in the body

One of the greatest weapons Satan has used against the church is division. Paul urged the Ephesian church:

> **Ephesians 4:3** *"Make every effort to keep the unity of the Spirit through the bond of peace."*

The church will not overcome any crisis if we remain divided by petty disputes, personal ambitions, prideful allegiances, True unity is not built on compromise but on a shared commitment to Christ, His mission, and His truth.

This does not mean that we ignore doctrinal differences or tolerate error. But it does mean that we always put love above personal preference; that we pursue reconciliation where there is conflict; and that we strive to build up rather than tear down. The church is strongest when it stands together in truth, love, and humility.

4. Rejecting fear and embracing faith

Discouragement and disillusionment often come because we focus more on the crisis than on Christ.

> **John 16:33** *"In this world you will have trouble. But take heart! I have overcome the world."*

Fear paralyses; faith mobilises. If we allow the challenges of our time to breed fear, we will retreat into complacency and self-preservation.

But if we choose faith, we will move forward in courage, confident that God is at work and that He will accomplish His purposes through His people.

This faith is not blind optimism but a firm trust in God's sovereignty. He has not abandoned His church, nor will He. His kingdom will not be shaken. The key question is not whether God is faithful but whether we will trust Him enough to step out in obedience.

5. Reviving a passion for evangelism

A church that is preoccupied with internal struggles often loses sight of the mission of Christ.

> **Matthew 28:19-20** *"Go and make disciples of all nations, baptizing them in the name of the Father and of the Son and of the Holy Spirit, and teaching them to obey everything I have commanded you."*

Evangelism is not an optional program; it is the lifeblood of the church. When we focus on those who don't know Christ, our internal distractions fade. When we engage in mission, our faith is strengthened. The church cannot afford to be inwardly focused – we must go out into the world, proclaim the gospel, and call people to salvation.

Every believer has a role in this mission. Whether through personal witness, supporting missions, or engaging in community outreach, we must recover the urgency of sharing the good news.

6. Remaining Faithful Until the End

In every generation, God has preserved a faithful remnant - those who refuse to compromise, who stand firm in truth, and who remain committed to the cause of Christ.

Revelation 2:10 *"Be faithful, even to the point of death, and I will give you life as your victor's crown."*

The future may bring more challenges, more opposition, and greater trials for the church. But God has called us to endure. He has promised that the gates of hell will not prevail against His church (Matthew 16:18). We do not fight for victory; we fight from victory. Christ has already won.

How then shall you live?

Will you remain passive, lamenting the state of the church without taking action? Or will you rise up, renewed in faith, committed to truth, and ready to engage in the battle before us?

The time for excuses has passed. The time for compromise has passed. The time for indecision has passed. The time for action is now.

Return to your first love.

Reclaim biblical truth.

Restore unity.

Reject fear and embrace faith.

Revive your passion for evangelism.

Remain faithful to the end.

The church is in crisis - but crisis is always an opportunity for renewal. May we be the generation that stands firm, that seeks God wholeheartedly, and that rises above the many challenges before us to shine the light of Christ into a dark world. The choice is yours.

It's decision time …

www.ingramcontent.com/pod-product-compliance
Lightning Source LLC
Chambersburg PA
CBHW071243020426

42333CB00015B/1599